2nd Edition

OVER

800

PRACTICE
QUESTIONS

07/16

6/4/18.

...eracy
...cy
...s

Chris Tyreman

KoganPage

First published in Great Britain by Kogan Page 2011
Second edition 2016

2nd Floor, 45 Gee Street
London
EC1V 3RS
United Kingdom

© Chris Tyreman 2011 and 2016

ISBN   978 0 7494 7829 2
E-ISBN   978 0 7494 7830 8

British Library Cataloguing-in-Publication Data

A CIP record for this book is available from the British Library.

Typeset by Graphicraft Limited, Hong Kong
Print production managed by Jellyfish
Printed and bound in Great Britain by CPI Group (UK) Ltd, Croydon CR0

Contents

Introduction 1

PART ONE
Numeracy 7

1 Mental arithmetic 9

Maths audit 1 9
Review of mental arithmetic 11
Understanding fractions 35
Understanding decimals 56
Calculating percentages 66
Time 70
Money 70
Speed, distance and time 71
Introduction to the mental arithmetic questions 83
Exemplar test with answers 84
Mental arithmetic tests 1–5 85

2 General arithmetic 91

Maths audit 2 91
How to round decimal numbers – decimal place (d.p.) 92
The metric system of measurement (SI units) 94
Areas, borders, perimeters and volumes 95
Scales 98
Aspects of algebra 98
Rearranging linear equations 99
Trends 100
Averages 100
Weighted average 102

3 Statistics 105

Maths audit 3 105
Pie charts 106
Bar charts 108
Line graphs 111
Scatter graphs 113
Tables 117
Tally charts, frequency tables and histograms 120
Cumulative frequency graphs 124
Box and whisker plots 128
Introduction to the 'on-screen'-type mock tests 130
Mock test 1 (16 'on-screen' questions in 35 minutes) 131
Mock test 2 (16 'on-screen' questions in 35 minutes) 139

PART TWO
Literacy 147

4 Spelling 149

Introduction 149
Rules of spelling 149
Spelling test 1: Double consonants (rules apply) 151
Spelling test 2: Double consonants (learn by heart) 152
Spelling test 3: 100 words to spell correctly 156
Spelling test 4: Word selection 159

5 Punctuation 163

Introduction 163
Problems with paragraphs 164
Problems with capital letters and full stops 164
Problems with commas 164
Problems with semi-colons and colons 166
Problems with the apostrophe and possession 166
Problems with contractions 167
Problems with speech marks and quotation marks 167
Problems with question marks 168
Problems with brackets (parentheses) 168
Punctuation test 1 169
Punctuation test 2 170
Punctuation test 3 171

6   Grammar 173

Introduction 173
Review of grammar 174
Grammar test 1 180
Sentence construction 182
Grammar test 2 184
Grammar test 3 185

7   Comprehension 187

Introduction 187

Comprehension passage 1 187
Task A: Choosing a main heading 188
Task B: Choosing a sub-heading 189
Task C: Comparing statements with the text 189
Task D: Choosing statements that express the meaning of text 190

Comprehension passage 2 190
Task E: Matching categories with statements 191
Task F: Choosing information from a list 192
Task G: Summarizing paragraphs in a sentence 192

Comprehension passage 3 193
Task H: Presenting the key points of the passage 193
Task I: Choosing the correct audience 194

Comprehension passage 4 194
Task J: Placing the key points in the correct sequence 195

PART THREE
Answers with explanations and Glossary 197

Answers 199
Numeracy 199
Literacy 236

Glossary 251
Numeracy 251
Literacy 254

Introduction

All trainee teachers seeking Qualified Teacher Status (QTS) must pass three computer-based tests in numeracy, literacy, and Information and Communications Technology (ICT). This book will enable you to pass the Numeracy QTS Skills Test and the Literacy QTS Skills Test at your first attempt. Of course it cannot, without some effort, miraculously pass these two tests for you, but if you work steadily through each chapter you can succeed.

Numeracy (Chapters 1–3)

The pass mark in the QTS Numeracy Skills Test is 18 correct answers out of 28 questions (63 per cent) and although this is not very high, slow candidates can lose too many marks to pass. For this reason, the first chapter teaches quick ways of answering the mental arithmetic questions. Five mock QTS mental arithmetic tests of 12 questions each provide plenty of practice.

The remaining two chapters cover the general arithmetic and statistical skills required for the 'on-screen' questions. Two mock 'on-screen' QTS-type tests complete the numeracy section of the book, which comes with worked-through answers.

Each chapter begins with a 'maths audit' so you can review the exact skills required for each section of the test. To interpret the questions you must be able to convert the language of the questions into mathematical operations, as per the following example:

> A comprehensive school has fourteen hundred pupils on roll, including
> one-hundred and fifty-four A-level students. What percentage of the pupils
> on roll are A-level students?

The arithmetic required is division followed by multiplication:

154 ÷ 1400 × 100%

All the material in this book comes with expanded answers that show the calculations.

While you need only to remember the four arithmetic operations of addition(+), subtraction(−), multiplication(×) and division(÷), you should be familiar with the different ways that these operations can be denoted in question form, as given here:

(×)   multiply by, times, lots of, product, twice, double, multiple, fraction;

(÷)   divide by, proportion, ratio, per/per cent, out of, half, each, scale, factor;

(+)   add, total, plus, sum, tally, more than;

(−)   subtract, difference, take, less than.

To interpret the graphs you must be able to work out the distance from one tick mark to the next along the axis, ie divide the scale by the number of tick mark intervals, as per the examples shown below:

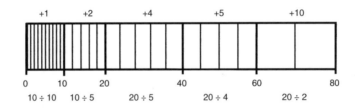

Students who fail the test tend to do so for the following reasons.

Lack of knowledge

This is probably the main reason why students fail. As a guide, you should have at least a grade B in GCSE Maths if you expect to pass the test without preparing for it. If you managed only a grade C or lower then you must prepare carefully. This book will help you whatever your level because it assumes that you have forgotten much of what you learnt at school or college, or that you never understood it in the first place. It builds on your existing knowledge by using graded exercises combined with fully explained answers. Mock tests are included to simulate the live test experience as far as possible.

Pressure of time

Time restraints are another key reason why candidates fail. The test lasts 48 minutes with 12 minutes for the mental arithmetic questions and 36 minutes for the longer on-screen questions. The mental arithmetic questions are the most troublesome because each question has a strict time limit. If you are only half way through a question when the next question is read out then you cannot put up your hand and ask the questioner to wait! With the on-screen questions you can work at your own pace even if the penalty is missing out on answering every question. It is better to be certain of a few correct answers than to guess too many, leaving everything to chance.

Another tip for improving your mark is to increase the speed of your calculations and the book explains ways in which this can be done. Do not attempt to work out every problem mentally but instead use the pencil and paper provided to write down most of the steps in a calculation. You are far more likely to make numerical errors if you rely too heavily on your memory. For the purposes of the QTS test, mental arithmetic is not about working everything out in your head, it is arithmetic without the help of a calculator.

Maths phobia

This is the third reason why people fail. Test takers with a mental block on maths are susceptible to panic attacks before or during the test and this can lead to repeated failures. Fortunately for these people, there is no limit on the number of times they can attempt to pass the QTS tests and gain Qualified Teacher Status. This third reason for lack of test success is really a combination of the first two, ie a lack of knowledge and an inability to cope with the pressure of working against the clock. A vicious circle of anxiety and a lack of understanding ensue to create even more anxiety with feelings of hopelessness. If this happens to you, then stop, put down your pencil, close your eyes, take a few deep breaths, then open your eyes and start again. Maths phobia can be overcome by practising your maths skills daily until you feel more confident.

Calculator skills

The calculator and the on-screen nature of the test can be off-putting for some people. You should not have to rely on the on-screen calculator for every single step of the on-screen questions, but you do need to make sure that you are confident with a calculator for the times when it is required. The QTS on-screen calculator is a basic arithmetic calculator rather than a scientific type. This means that it will only cope with single-step arithmetic processes, eg 250 ÷ 1.6 is fine. You simply use the mouse to click on [2] [5] [0] [÷] [1] [.] [6] [=] . However, 250 ÷ 1.6 + 2.75 must be manually split into two parts: 250 ÷ 1.6 = 156.25 (write the answer down), then click on [C] to clear the answer and use the mouse to enter 156.25 + 2.75 as a final step, ie [1] [5] [6] [.] [2] [5] [+] [2] [.] [7] [5] . The [CE] key can be used to clear the last entry if you make a mistake but it is often better to use the [C] key and start the calculation afresh. Finally, you can click on the blue bar at the head of the calculator to drag it to a more convenient position on the screen.

Literacy (Chapters 4–7)

The pass mark in the QTS Literacy Skills Test is 30 correct answers out of 48 questions (63 per cent). You have 45 minutes to complete the test, or just less than one minute per question, which should be sufficient time for most candidates. The test is 'on-screen' and through headphones and it checks spelling, punctuation, grammar and comprehension. This book has one chapter to cover each of these skills, with practice questions that check basic literacy and QTS-level skills.

Revision

Student teachers are assumed to have a basic degree of literacy so each chapter sets out to encourage candidates to develop skills that they already have. In the spelling section, for example, the 'rules of spelling' are reviewed and two tests boost confidence in those words that candidates find difficult to spell. Almost one-third of the exam marks come from the punctuation section of the test. All the important punctuation marks are reviewed along with their correct (✓) and incorrect application (✗); right and wrong symbols are also used throughout the punctuation, grammar and comprehension sections to facilitate quicker revision of the right answer and how to avoid common failings.

The grammar chapter of the book checks your ability to write grammatically correct sentences as well as to identify grammatical errors. Two tests are used to identify weak areas in word selection and sentence construction. The comprehension chapter includes four passages with QTS-style questions and expanded answers where necessary.

Technique

In the spelling test you have to click on an icon to hear a word through headphones, before typing the correct spelling into a blank space. You can click on the icon again to hear the word more times if you wish. Each word is in the context of a sentence, which helps to clarify the spelling. Once you have finished this section of the test you cannot go back to it later on. However, you can move forwards and backwards through the remaining three sections, which do not require headphones.

In the punctuation test you need to double-click on the word that requires punctuation adding; the word is then highlighted and an edit box appears to enable you to add (or amend) the punctuation before clicking the OK button. If you make a mistake or change your mind then you can click the Cancel or Reset buttons in the edit box. To start a new paragraph you highlight (double-click) the last word in the previous sentence and then click on the 'P' button in the edit box followed by OK. It is not always necessary to add punctuation to a sentence, but you will need to show consistency throughout the text.

In the grammar test you have to drag and drop into place the correct ending to a sentence from the four choices available, for example, the ending that contains the correct verb tense or the appropriate verb–noun agreement.

The comprehension test is multiple-choice. Depending on the question, you might have to drag a tick symbol (✓) into the answer box to indicate your choice, or it could be a letter, eg M (most), L (least), or it could be an abbreviation or acronym, eg DfE (Department for Education). Answer the questions you find the easiest first.

TDA website

You can register for the QTS skills tests via the following web address: www.skillstestbooking.com (or type QTS into the Google search engine). To book a test you will need a registration number issued to you by your training provider. Full details of where to take the tests are available from the TDA website which includes links to on-line practice tests. You can book all three QTS tests for the same day if there is the availability. Your test results will be shown on-screen as soon as you have finished the tests.

Part one

Numeracy

Chapter 1

Mental arithmetic

Maths audit 1

For the mental arithmetic section you need to know the following.

Whole numbers

- How to add, subtract, multiply and divide whole numbers.

- How to multiply by or divide by 10, 100, 1000, etc.

- How to break down large numbers by finding the prime factors.

Fractions, proportions and ratios

- How to add and subtract fractions with the same and different denominators (find a common denominator).

- How to multiply fractions together (multiply the top numbers and the bottom numbers).

- How to divide fractions (turn the right-hand fraction upside down and multiply as for multiplications).

- How to work with improper (top-heavy) fractions (same rules apply).

- How to work with mixed fractions (whole number + fraction) by converting to an improper fraction as a first step.

- How to cancel fractions (equivalent fractions) and cross-cancel fractions when multiplying fractions together.

- How to divide quantities into ratios and proportional parts.

Decimal numbers

- How to add and subtract decimal numbers (same as for whole numbers but keep the decimal points aligned).

- How to multiply decimals by 10, 100, 1000, etc (move the decimal point to the right by how many zeros you have).

- How to divide decimals by 10, 100, 1000, etc (move the decimal point to the left by how many zeros you have).

- How to multiply decimals by ordinary numbers (multiply as normal and then remember: number of decimal places in the question = number of decimal places in the answer).

- How to divide decimals by ordinary numbers (divide as normal keeping the decimal point in the same position).

- How to divide by decimal numbers (change the decimal into a whole number as a first step).

- How to convert decimals into fractions and vice versa.

Percentages

- How to express a percentage as a fraction with a denominator of 100.

- How to write a percentage as a decimal by dividing by 100.

- How to multiply any number by any percentage using either a fractions method or a decimals method.

- How to work out a percentage change (increase or decrease).

Time

- How to express time using the 24-hour clock.

- How to calculate time intervals, and find start and end times.

Money

● How to work with the decimal system and exchange rates.

Speed, distance and time

● How to calculate speed knowing distance and time.

● How to calculate distance knowing speed and time.

● How to calculate time knowing distance and speed.

Review of mental arithmetic

Place value

Large numbers (greater than nine) are built up with separate columns for hundreds, tens and units. Each column can have numbers ranging from nought to nine (0 to 9), but the value of each number in the column has a different meaning. The table below lists some numbers in words with their corresponding figures and place values:

Number in words	Number in figures*			
	TH	H	T	U
two hundred and six		2	0	6
five hundred and sixty-four		5	6	4
six hundred and thirty-two		6	3	2
six thousand two hundred	6	2	0	0

* TH = thousands; H = hundreds; T = tens; U = units

The figure 6 (underlined) has a different place value depending on which column it appears in. It can mean 6, 60, 600 or 6000:

In 206 the six means six UNITS (6 × 1 = 6).
In 564 the six means six TENS (6 × 10 = 60).
In 632 the six means six HUNDREDS (6 × 100 = 600).
In 6200 the six means six THOUSANDS (6 × 1000 = 6000).

Very large numbers are built up in the same way as for smaller numbers with columns for tens of thousands, hundreds of thousands and millions. For example:

200128 is two hundred thousand one hundred and twenty-eight.

1150235 is one million one hundred and fifty thousand two hundred and thirty-five.

Place values can be used to make simple mental arithmetic calculations without a pen and paper and to solve more complex calculations without the need for a calculator. The following questions are based on the simple concept of place value but in some instances they do require a little thought!

1 Warm-up exercise

1   Write 2540 in words.   *Answer* ....

2   In words, what is the place value of the underlined number in 25<u>4</u>0?

     Answer ....

3   In words, what is the place value of 0 in 2540?

     Answer ....

4   In words, what is the place value of 0 in 2045?

     Answer ....

5   In numbers, what is the place value of 1 in 515400?

     Answer ....

6   In numbers, what is the place value of 5 in 512400?

     Answer ....

7   Rearrange the figures in 34529 to give the largest possible number.

     Answer ....

8   Rearrange the figures in 34529 to give the smallest possible number.

     Answer ....

9   Write 51240000 in words.   *Answer* ....

10   In numbers and words, what is the place value of 5 in 51240000?

     Answer ....

The four processes of arithmetic

Addition

Traditionally numbers have been arranged underneath each other so that the units, tens and hundreds columns etc are kept in vertical alignment.

   Example: 139 + 226

We align the numbers in columns and then add the units column (right-hand column) giving $6 + 9 = 15$.

The number five is placed in the units column and the number ten is carried over as one 'ten' into the tens column.

```
H  T  U
1  3  9
2  2  6  +
_____
      5
_____
   1
```

Now we add the tens column (middle column, remembering to include the 'one' that has been carried: $1 + 2 + 3 = 6$ (middle column):

```
1  3  9
2  2  6  +
_____
   6  5
_____
   1
```

Now we add the hundreds column: $2 + 1 = 3$ (left-hand column):

```
1  3  9
2  2  6  +
_____
3  6  5
_____
   1
```

For the addition of three or more numbers, the method is the same. For example, $200 + 86 + 44$ becomes

```
2  0  0
   8  6
   4  4  +
_____
3  3  0
_____
1  1
```

Subtraction

Subtraction is concerned with taking things away. Subtraction is the reverse of addition. The most important thing about subtraction is that the larger number is on top (above the smaller), so when subtracting you subtract the smaller number from the larger number.

As with addition, the numbers must be arranged underneath each other, so that the units, tens and hundreds columns are in line. After aligning the numbers, we subtract (take away) the columns vertically, starting at the right-hand end (units column). For example:

374 – 126

The first step is to align the numbers in columns with the larger number above the smaller number:

```
H  T  U
3  7  4
1  2  6  –
```

The next step is to subtract the units (right-hand column), 4 – 6, which we cannot do since six is larger than four.

To overcome this problem we borrow one from the tens column (this is the same as ten units) and add it to the four in the units column. So our sum now becomes:

14 – 6 (we can do) = 8

So far we can write:

```
3  7  ¹4
1  2  6  –
_____
      8
_____
```

The next step is to pay back the 'one' we have just borrowed from the tens column. There are two methods for doing this and both are now explained.

Method 1 (traditional method)
In this method the ten is paid back to the bottom. For example:

```
3  7   ¹4
1  2¹  6  –
_____
       8
_____
```

Now we add the 1 and the 2 to make 3. The 3 is subtracted from the 7 to give to the 4. So the sum becomes:

$$
\begin{array}{ccc}
3 & 7 & {}^{1}4 \\
1 & 2^{1} & 6 \\
\hline
 & 4 & 8
\end{array}\ -
$$

Finally we subtract the 1 from 3 (in the hundreds column) to give 2:

$$
\begin{array}{ccc}
3 & 7 & {}^{1}4 \\
1 & 2^{1} & 6 \\
\hline
2 & 4 & 8
\end{array}\ -
$$

Method 2 (modern method)

In this method the ten borrowed is subtracted as a one at the top of the tens column $(7 - 1 = 6)$:

$$
\begin{array}{ccc}
3 & 7^{6_1} & 4 \\
1 & 2 & 6 \\
\hline
2 & 4 & 8
\end{array}\ -
$$

Now try the following questions. *You must not use a calculator* for any questions in this book, except for the purposes of checking answers.

2 *Warm-up exercise*

Work out the following additions and subtractions:

1   472 + 24   *Answer* ....

2   178 + 35   *Answer* ....

3   2830 + 250 + 67   *Answer* ....

4   957 − 340   *Answer* ....

5   1327 − 898   *Answer* ....

6   375 − 123   *Answer* ....

7   375 − 123 − 38   *Answer* ....

8   375 − 123 + 59   *Answer* ....

Multiplication

Multiplication (or 'times') means 'lots of' and is a quick way of adding up numbers that have the same value. For example:

```
3
3
3
3
3+      5 lots of 3
15      5 × 3 = 15 (5 times 3 equals 15)
```

Note that 5 × 3 = 15 and also 3 × 5 equals 15:

```
3        5
3        5
3        5+
3        15
3+
15
```

This applies to all numbers that are multiplied together; it does not matter which way around you put them, the answer is the same. The answer 15 is known as the 'product' of 5 and 3 (or 3 and 5). To multiply two numbers you need to be familiar with your 'Times Tables' up to 10 by 10 (up to 12 by 12 is better). It is essential that you memorize these tables because calculators are not allowed in the examination room.

Multiplication table (try to memorize to at least 10 × 10)

	1	2	3	4	5	6	7	8	9	10	11	12
1	1	2	3	4	5	6	7	8	9	10	11	12
2	2	4	6	8	10	12	14	16	18	20	22	24
3	3	6	9	12	15	18	21	24	27	30	33	36
4	4	8	12	16	20	24	28	32	36	40	44	48
5	5	10	15	20	25	30	35	40	45	50	55	60
6	6	12	18	24	30	36	42	48	54	60	66	72
7	7	14	21	28	35	42	49	56	63	70	77	84
8	8	16	24	32	40	48	56	64	72	80	88	96
9	9	18	27	36	45	54	63	72	81	90	99	108
10	10	20	30	40	50	60	70	80	90	100	110	120
11	11	22	33	44	55	66	77	88	99	110	121	132
12	12	24	36	48	60	72	84	96	108	120	132	144

The common times tables

2 times	3 times	4 times	5 times	6 times	7 times
$1 \times 2 = 2$	$1 \times 3 = 3$	$1 \times 4 = 4$	$1 \times 5 = 5$	$1 \times 6 = 6$	$1 \times 7 = 7$
$2 \times 2 = 4$	$2 \times 3 = 6$	$2 \times 4 = 8$	$2 \times 5 = 10$	$2 \times 6 = 12$	$2 \times 7 = 14$
$3 \times 2 = 6$	$3 \times 3 = 9$	$3 \times 4 = 12$	$3 \times 5 = 15$	$3 \times 6 = 18$	$3 \times 7 = 21$
$4 \times 2 = 8$	$4 \times 3 = 12$	$4 \times 4 = 16$	$4 \times 5 = 20$	$4 \times 6 = 24$	$4 \times 7 = 28$
$5 \times 2 = 10$	$5 \times 3 = 15$	$5 \times 4 = 20$	$5 \times 5 = 25$	$5 \times 6 = 30$	$5 \times 7 = 35$
$6 \times 2 = 12$	$6 \times 3 = 18$	$6 \times 4 = 24$	$6 \times 5 = 30$	$6 \times 6 = 36$	$6 \times 7 = 42$
$7 \times 2 = 14$	$7 \times 3 = 21$	$7 \times 4 = 28$	$7 \times 5 = 35$	$7 \times 6 = 42$	$7 \times 7 = 49$
$8 \times 2 = 16$	$8 \times 3 = 24$	$8 \times 4 = 32$	$8 \times 5 = 40$	$8 \times 6 = 48$	$8 \times 7 = 56$
$9 \times 2 = 18$	$9 \times 3 = 27$	$9 \times 4 = 36$	$9 \times 5 = 45$	$9 \times 6 = 54$	$9 \times 7 = 63$
$10 \times 2 = 20$	$10 \times 3 = 30$	$10 \times 4 = 40$	$10 \times 5 = 50$	$10 \times 6 = 60$	$10 \times 7 = 70$
$11 \times 2 = 22$	$11 \times 3 = 33$	$11 \times 4 = 44$	$11 \times 5 = 55$	$11 \times 6 = 66$	$11 \times 7 = 77$
$12 \times 2 = 24$	$12 \times 3 = 36$	$12 \times 4 = 48$	$12 \times 5 = 60$	$12 \times 6 = 72$	$12 \times 7 = 84$

8 times	9 times	10 times	11 times	12 times
$1 \times 8 = 8$	$1 \times 9 = 9$	$1 \times 10 = 10$	$1 \times 11 = 11$	$1 \times 12 = 12$
$2 \times 8 = 16$	$2 \times 9 = 18$	$2 \times 10 = 20$	$2 \times 11 = 22$	$2 \times 12 = 24$
$3 \times 8 = 24$	$3 \times 9 = 27$	$3 \times 10 = 30$	$3 \times 11 = 33$	$3 \times 12 = 36$
$4 \times 8 = 32$	$4 \times 9 = 36$	$4 \times 10 = 40$	$4 \times 11 = 44$	$4 \times 12 = 48$
$5 \times 8 = 40$	$5 \times 9 = 45$	$5 \times 10 = 50$	$5 \times 11 = 55$	$5 \times 12 = 60$
$6 \times 8 = 48$	$6 \times 9 = 54$	$6 \times 10 = 60$	$6 \times 11 = 66$	$6 \times 12 = 72$
$7 \times 8 = 56$	$7 \times 9 = 63$	$7 \times 10 = 70$	$7 \times 11 = 77$	$7 \times 12 = 84$
$8 \times 8 = 64$	$8 \times 9 = 72$	$8 \times 10 = 80$	$8 \times 11 = 88$	$8 \times 12 = 96$
$9 \times 8 = 72$	$9 \times 9 = 81$	$9 \times 10 = 90$	$9 \times 11 = 99$	$9 \times 12 = 108$
$10 \times 8 = 80$	$10 \times 9 = 90$	$10 \times 10 = 100$	$10 \times 11 = 110$	$10 \times 12 = 120$
$11 \times 8 = 88$	$11 \times 9 = 99$	$11 \times 10 = 110$	$11 \times 11 = 121$	$11 \times 12 = 132$
$12 \times 8 = 96$	$12 \times 9 = 108$	$12 \times 10 = 120$	$12 \times 11 = 132$	$12 \times 12 = 144$

Short multiplication

Multiplication of any number by a unit (1 to 9), for example: 6×5; 68×9; 390×7; 5240×3.

Example: what is 68×9? We rewrite this as:

```
6   8
    9   ×
```

Multiplying the units gives $8 \times 9 = 72$ (see nine times table), so we have:

```
6   8
    9  ×
─────────
    2
─────────
    7
```

We multiply the 6 in the tens column by the 9 to give $6 \times 9 = 54$.

The 54 is added to the 7 previously carried, to give $54 + 7 = 61$. The 1 of the 61 is placed in the tens column and the 6 of the 61 is carried into the hundreds column:

```
    6   8
        9  ×
─────────────
    1   2
6   7
```

Since there are no hundreds to multiply in the hundreds column, the figure 6 can be carried directly into this column, giving:

```
    6   8
        9  ×
─────────────
6   1   2
6   7
```

3 *Warm-up exercise*

1	7×9	*Answer* ....
2	12×8	*Answer* ....
3	11×12	*Answer* ....
4	Multiply 20 by 6	*Answer* ....
5	Multiply 23 by 4	*Answer* ....
6	90 times 5	*Answer* ....
7	The product of 19 and 5	*Answer* ....
8	33×3	*Answer* ....
9	75×4	*Answer* ....
10	125×8	*Answer* ....

Long multiplication

Multiplying any number by a number greater than 9, eg 52 × 18; 120 × 50 etc. To multiply 52 × 18 we rewrite this as:

```
  5   2
  1   8  ×
_____
_____
```

We proceed in two steps as follows: first by multiplying the 52 by the 8 in the units column and second by multiplying the 52 by the 1 in the tens column.

First step: (multiply 52 by the 8) so we have:

```
      5   2
      1   8  ×
_____
  4   1   6
      1
_____
```

Second step: (multiply the 52 by the 1 in the tens column). Since we are now multiplying from the tens column we leave the units column blank which is the same as filling it with a 0. The sum is written on the line below 416.

```
      5   2
      1   8  ×
_____
  4   1   6
  5   2   0
```

We now add the two steps together, ie add 416 and 520 to give the final sum which is shown below:

```
      5   2
      1   8  ×
_____
  4   1   6
  5   2   0  +
_____
  9   3   6
_____
```

4 Warm-up exercise

Work out the following multiplication sums:

1   62 × 13   *Answer* ....

2   79 × 32   *Answer* ....

3   80 × 15   *Answer* ....

4   254 × 20   *Answer* ....

5   17 × 25   *Answer* ....

6   125 × 80   *Answer* ....

7   167 × 33   *Answer* ....

8   42 × 121   *Answer* ....

Multiplication by 10, 100 and 1000

To multiply a number by ten we add a nought to the number, for example: $5 \times 10 = 50$. This has the effect of moving the number one along to the left in the hundreds, tens and units columns (increasing its value ten times).

```
H  T  U                      H  T  U
      5   × 10      =               5  0
```

Multiplication by 100 is the same except that you add two zeros. This moves the number two places to the left.

Example: $3 \times 100 = 300$:

```
H  T  U                      H  T  U
      3   × 100     =         3  0  0
```

and $12 \times 100 = 1200$:

```
TH  H  T  U                  TH  H  T  U
       1  2  × 100   =       1   2  0  0
```

(ie twelve hundred is one thousand two hundred)

To multiply by 1000 we add three zeros, so $8 \times 1000 = 8000$

```
TH  H  T  U                  TH  H  T  U
       8  × 1000    =        8   0  0  0
```

18 × 1000 = 18000 (eighteen thousand):

TTH	TH	H	T	U			TTH	TH	H	T	U
		1	8	× 1000	=		1	8	0	0	0

In this case we have to go to the next column along – the tens of thousands column (TTH) – to give one ten thousand. Together with the eight thousands it gives us eighteen thousand.

5 Warm-up exercise

Work out the following multiplication by adding noughts (zeros):

1   28 × 10   *Answer* ....

2   6 × 1000   *Answer* ....

3   49 × 10   *Answer* ....

4   49 × 100   *Answer* ....

5   49 × 1000   *Answer* ....

Division

Division is the reverse of multiplication and is concerned with sharing (or dividing numbers into equal parts). For example, divide 195 by 3, ie 195 ÷ 3. We rewrite as follows:

$$3\overline{)195}$$

The first step is to divide the 1 by the 3. However, since 3 into 1 won't go, we have to carry the 1 into the next column:

$3\overline{)1^195}$ giving us 3 into 19

We now use the multiplication table in reverse to find how many 3s are in 19. To do this, start in the 3s column on the left-hand side and move along the horizontal row until you get to the number which is closest to but smaller than 19. The number is 18. Following the vertical row upwards gives us 6. So 3 goes into 19 six times with 1 left over (19 – 18 = 1[left over]). The 6 is placed at the top; the 1 is carried to the next column to make 15:

$$\frac{6}{3\overline{)1^19^15}}$$

Finally the 3 is divided into 15. The three times table shows us that 3 goes into 15 times exactly five times, so the finished sum is:

$$3{\overline{)1^19^15}}\quad 6\,5$$

So $195 \div 3 = 65$. The answer can be checked by multiplying it by the number that we have divided by ($65 \times 3 = 195$ – correct). The answer (65) is known as the *quotient*. The number we are dividing by (3) is the *divisor*, and the number we are dividing into (195) is the *dividend*. Note that if the dividend had been 196 instead of 195 then the answer would have been 65 *remainder* 1 (65 with 1 left over).

6 Warm-up exercise

Work out the following divisions:

1 $36 \div 9$ *Answer* ....

2 $248 \div 4$ *Answer* ....

3 $3{\overline{)339}}$ *Answer* ....

4 $5{\overline{)265}}$ *Answer* ....

5 $1230 \div 3$ *Answer* ....

6 $295 \div 5$ *Answer* ....

7 $1464 \div 6$ *Answer* ....

8 $1000 \div 8$ *Answer* ....

Long division (division by large numbers)
For example, 2064 divided by 48.

We write: $48{\overline{)2064}}$

First step: divide 2 by 48 – won't go
Second step: divide 20 by 48 – won't go
Third step: divide 206 by 48 – will go

48 into 206 will go, but we don't have a times table for 48 so we have to *build up a table ourselves*. This is done as follows:

$1 \times 48 = 48$
$2 \times 48 = 96$ $4 \times 48 = 192$ (the nearest to 206)
$3 \times 48 = 144$ $5 \times 48 = 240$ (too big)

Fourth step: work out the remainder. We know that 48 goes into 206 four times to leave a remainder of 14 (206 – 192).

$$\begin{array}{r} 4 \\ 48\overline{)2064} \\ 192- \\ \hline 14 \end{array}$$

Fifth step: we now bring the 4 down to give 144:

$$\begin{array}{r} 4 \\ 48\overline{)2064} \\ 192- \\ \hline 144 \end{array}$$

Sixth step: the 48 is divided into 144 to give 3 with no remainder (see 48 times table on the previous page)

$$\begin{array}{r} 43 \\ 48\overline{)2064} \\ 192- \\ \hline 144 \\ 144- \end{array}$$

So 2064 ÷ 48 = 43.

7 *Warm-up exercise*

Work out the following long divisions:

1   360 ÷ 12   *Answer* ....

2   372 ÷ 12   *Answer* ....

3   18$\overline{)792}$ *Answer* ....

4   20$\overline{)900}$ *Answer* ....

5   72$\overline{)1440}$ *Answer* ....

6   216 ÷ 36   *Answer* ....

7   950 ÷ 25   *Answer* ....

8   2680 ÷ 40   *Answer* ....

9   976 ÷ 16   *Answer* ....

10   4944 ÷ 24   *Answer* ....

Law of operations ('BIDMAS')

The order of working out problems is:

B = Brackets;
I = Indices;
D = Division;
M = Multiplication;
A = Addition;
S = Subtraction.

There is a definite order in which to work out a sum containing more than one arithmetic sign. The rule is: brackets first followed by indices (powers) then division or multiplication and finally addition or subtraction. For example:

$4 \times 3 + 6$

Multiplication first: $4 \times 3 = 12$ followed by addition: $12 + 6 = 18$.

So $4 \times 3 + 6 = 18$.

If we carried out the addition part first $(3 + 6 = 9)$ and then multiplied by the 4, this would have given 36 $(4 \times 9 = 36)$ which is the wrong answer. For example:

$25 - 12 \div 3$

Division first: $12 \div 3 = 4$ followed by subtraction $25 - 4 = 21$.

So $25 - 12 \div 3 = 21$.

Where a calculation contains *only* addition and subtraction then each part is worked out in a sequence from left to right. For example:

$11 - 3 + 9 - 2$ becomes $11 - 3 = 8$ then $8 + 9 = 17$ then finally $17 - 2 = 15$.

Where a calculation contains only multiplication and division then each part is worked out *in sequence* from left to right. For example:

$10 \div 2 \times 6$ becomes $10 \div 2 = 5$ followed by $5 \times 6 = 30$.

8 *Warm-up exercise*

Work out the following (without using a calculator):

1 $12 \div 6 + 12$ *Answer* ....

2 $10 + 15 \div 5$ *Answer* ....

3 $3 \times 4 - 2$ *Answer* ....

4 $8 - 3 \times 2$ *Answer* ....

5 $10 + 20 \div 5$ *Answer* ....

6 $15 - 9 + 3$ *Answer* ....

7 $14 + 11 - 10 - 6$ *Answer* ....

8 $22 \times 4 \div 2 + 12$ *Answer* ....

9 $30 \div 6 \times 5 - 15$ *Answer* ....

10 $2 \times 3 \times 4 \times 5 \div 20$ *Answer* ....

11 $10 - 1 \times 3 - 1$ *Answer* ....

12 $9 + 3 \times 4 \div 2 - 1$ *Answer* ....

Some calculations include brackets to help to make sure that the arithmetic is carried out in the correct sequence. Where a calculation contains *brackets* then the sum inside the brackets must be worked out before anything else. For example:

$12 \div (6 - 2)$

First step: $(6 - 2) = 4$
Second step: $12 \div 4 = 3$
So $12 \div (6 - 2) = 3$
Without the brackets, $12 \div 6 - 2$ is $12 \div 6 = 2$, then $2 - 2 = 0$

When no arithmetic sign is placed outside the brackets then the calculation is *automatically taken as being times ('×')*.

So $9(6 + 5)$ means $9 \times (6 + 5)$ giving $9 \times 11 = 99$

The sequence of operations is **BIDMAS: B**rackets first, then *****Indices, D**ivision or **M**ultiplication, and finally **A**ddition or **S**ubtraction (* eg squares and cubes, covered later).

9 *Warm-up exercise*

Calculate the following by working out the brackets first:

1 $9 + (5 \times 3)$ *Answer* ....

2 $14 - (10 + 2)$ *Answer* ....

3 $30 \div (3 \times 2)$ *Answer* ....

4 $4 \times (20 - 9)$ *Answer* ....

5 $10(10 - 9)$ *Answer* ....

6 $7 (15 \div 5)$ *Answer* ....

7 $3(10 + 6 \div 2)$ *Answer* ....

8 $3 + 6(4 \times 2 + 1)$ *Answer* ....

9 $2(23 - 17) \div 4$ *Answer* ....

10 $4 + 4(4 + 4)$ *Answer* ....

11 $90 \div 9(8 - 3 \times 2)$ *Answer* ....

12 $10 \times 2(60 \div 2 \times 15)$ *Answer* ....

Factors and multiples

The ability to break down (factorize) large numbers into smaller more manageable numbers, or factors, is an essential part of cancelling fractions. Factors and multiples are also useful for mental arithmetic calculations as discussed in a later chapter.

Factors are numbers that will divide into another number exactly, without leaving a remainder. A *divisor* is any number that you are dividing by; a divisor is a factor when it leaves no remainder. For example:

15 is a factor of 60 (60 divided by $15 = 4$)
50 is a factor of 250 (250 divided by $50 = 5$)
100 is a factor of 1000 (1000 divided by $100 = 10$)

All the factors of a number are all of the whole numbers that will divide into it exactly. Take the number 36, for example. The factors of 36 are:

1 and 36;
2 and 18;
3 and 12;
4 and 9;
6 and 6.

Notice how the factors are found in pairs; pairing off in this way will help you to find the factors of large numbers, without missing any out. The factors of 36 can be listed as:

1 2 3 4 6 9 12, 18 and 36

The highest common factor (HCF) of two numbers is the highest of their common factors. For example: what is the highest common factor of 60 and 15?

15: factors = 1 3 5 15 (by pairing off)
60: factors = 1 2 3 4 5 6 10 12 15 20 30 60

The factors that are common to both 15 and 60 are:

1 3 5 15 and of these 15 is the highest, so 15 is the HCF of 60 and 15.

Example: what is the HCF of 16 and 20?

16: 1 2 4 8 16
20: 1 2 4 5 10 20

1, 2 and 4 are the common factors so 4 is the HCF of 16 and 20.

Finding factors

When looking for factors, the following tests can be applied to whole numbers (integers):

i) If the *last* digit is 0, 2, 4, 6, or 8 (ie it is an even number) then the number will divide by 2. For example, 576 will divide by 2 because 6 will divide by 2.

ii) If the *last* digit is 1, 3, 5, 7, or 9 (ie it is an odd number) then the number will not divide by 2 without leaving a remainder. For example, 575 will not divide by 2 without leaving a remainder (so 2 is not a factor of 575).

iii) If the *sum* of the digits is 3 the number will divide by 3. For example, 576 will divide by 3 because $5 + 7 + 6 = 18$ and 18 is divisible by 3.

iv) If the *last two* digits are divisible by 4 the number is divisible by 4. For example, 128, 132, 136, 240, 244, 348, 552, 760, 964, 1012 etc.

v) If the *last* digit ends in 0 or 5 the number will divide by 5. For example, 1365 will divide by 5 because 65 will divide by 5; if you double a number ending in 5 it will divide by 10 (see vii).

vi) If the *sum* of the digits divides by 9 the number will divide by 9 (and also by 3 because 9 divides by 3). For example, 3474 will divide by 9 because $3 + 4 + 7 + 4 = 18$ and 18 is divisible by 9.

vii) If the last digit ends in 0 the number will divide by 10; if the last two digits are 00 the number will divide by 100 (and by 10), etc.

10 *Warm-up exercise*

Find the factors of the following numbers. Use the pairing-off method (1 and; 2 and; 3 and; 4 and; 5 and; 6 and; etc).

1   6 (four factors)   *Answer* ....

2   10 (four factors)   *Answer* ....

3   32 (six factors)   *Answer* ....

4   90 (twelve factors)   *Answer* ....

5   500 (twelve factors)   *Answer* ....

Find the highest common factor (HCF) of:

6   24 and 32   *Answer* ....

7   75 and 120   *Answer* ....

8   12 and 500   *Answer* ....

A *prime number* is a number that is *only* divisible by itself and one; a prime number has only two factors – the number itself and one. The lowest prime number is 2 (1 is not a prime number because it has only one factor – itself).

All the prime numbers below 50 are listed below:

2   3   5   7   11   13   17   19   23   29   31   37   41   43   47

Note: with the exception of 2, all the prime numbers are odd numbers (but not all odd numbers are prime numbers).

A factor that is a prime number is called a *prime factor*. To find the prime factors of any number we keep dividing by prime numbers – starting with the lowest prime number that will divide into it, and then progressing through until it will not divide by any prime number any further.

Example: what are the prime factors of 210?

$$210 \div 2 = 105$$
$$105 \div 3 = 35$$
$$35 \div 5 = 7$$
$$7 \div 7 = 1$$

So: 210 has the prime factors 2, 3, 5 and 7

$210 = 2 \times 3 \times 5 \times 7$

Example: express 2520 as a product of its prime factors.

As in the previous example we start dividing by the lowest prime number which is 2:

$2520 \div 2 = 1260$

1260 is an even number so it will divide by 2 again:

$1260 \div 2 = 630$

630 is an even number so it will divide by 2 again:

$630 \div 2 = 315$

315 is an odd number so it will not divide by 2 but it will divide by the next prime number which is 3:

$315 \div 3 = 105$

105 will divide by 3 again:

$105 \div 3 = 35$

35 will not divide by 3, but it will divide by the next prime number which is 5:

$35 \div 5 = 7$

7 is a prime number so it will not divide any further.

$7 \div 7 = 1$

So: $2520 = 2 \times 2 \times 2 \times 3 \times 3 \times 5 \times 7$

Note: finding the correct prime factors may involve 'trial and error' if the number is not divisible by the first prime factor you try.

$209 \div 2 = 104$ remainder 1, so 2 *is not* a prime factor of 209
$209 \div 3 = 69$ remainder 2, so 3 *is not* a prime factor of 209
$209 \div 5 = 41$ remainder 4, so 5 *is not* a prime factor of 209
$209 \div 7 = 29$ remainder 6, so 7 *is not* a prime factor of 209
$209 \div 11 = 19$ exactly so 11 is a prime factor of 209

From this we can see that 209 has the prime factors 11 and 19.

11 Warm-up exercise

Express the following numbers as a product of their prime factors (2, 3, 5, 7 etc):

1	6	*Answer*	**5**	81	*Answer* ....
2	30	*Answer*	**6**	216	*Answer* ....
3	63	*Answer*	**7**	125	*Answer* ....
4	420	*Answer*	**8**	343	*Answer* ....

A *multiple* of a number is the number multiplied by:

    1 2 3 4 5 6 7 8 9 10 11 12 13 14 etc.

So a multiple is the 'times table' of a number. For example:

    the multiples of 5 are: 5   10   15   20   25   30 etc.
    the multiples of 6 are: 6   12   18   24   30 etc.
    the multiples of 10 are: 10   20   30   40   50 etc.

Common multiples are those numbers which are common to a pair of numbers. For example: what are the first three common multiples of 5 and 10?

    multiples of 5:   5   10   15   20   25   30
    multiples of 10:   10   20   30   40   50

The common numbers are underlined; so the first three common multiples of 5 and 10 are: 10, 20 and 30. The lowest of these is 10, making it the lowest common multiple (LCM); it is the lowest number that both 5 and 10 will divide into exactly.

Example: find the LCM of 3 and 9:

    multiples of 3:   3   6   9   12   18
    multiples of 9:   9   18   27   36   45

so the LCM of 3 and 9 is 9

Example: find the LCM of 4 and 5:

    4:    4   8   12   16   20   24
    5:    5   10   15   20   25

so the LCM of 4 and 5 is 20

12 Warm-up exercise

Find the first four multiples of:

1 2   *Answer* ....

2 12   *Answer* ....

3 20   *Answer* ....

4 25   *Answer* ....

5 100   *Answer* ....

Find the lowest common multiple (LCM) of:

6   2 and 3   *Answer* ....

7   12 and 20   *Answer* ....

8   24 and 36   *Answer* ....

9   30 and 75   *Answer* ....

10 25 and 40   *Answer* ....

Rounding numbers

When rounding numbers we increase or decrease the answer to a sum to give the level of *accuracy* we want. For example, we can round answers to the nearest whole number, the nearest ten, the nearest hundred, the nearest thousand etc with any smaller numbers discarded (replaced with zeros).

To do this, you look at the column to the right of the column you are rounding to. If the number in that column is '5 or more' you round up and if it is less than 5 you round down. So 1, 2, 3, and 4 all round down, whereas 5, 6, 7, 8 and 9 all round up.

Example: work out 49×21 and round your answer to i) the nearest 10; ii) the nearest 100.

i) $49 \times 21 = 1029$. To round 1029 to the nearest ten you look at the column to the right of the tens column (ie the 9 units). This number is '5 or more' so you increase the number in the *tens column* by one to 3 (three tens is the nearest ten). So 1029 to the nearest ten is 1030.

ii)   49 × 21 = 1029. To round 1029 to the nearest hundred you look at the column to the right of the hundreds column (ie the two tens). This number is less than 5 so the number in the *hundreds column* remains the same ie 0 (no hundreds is the nearest hundred). So 1029 to the nearest hundred is 1000. The up/down split occurs at 1049. Numbers above 1049 round up to 1100, whereas numbers of 1049 and below round to 1000.

Example: round 82743 to i) the nearest ten; ii) nearest hundred; iii) nearest thousand.

i)   82743 – the 3 is less than 5 so the 4 remains the same (four tens) ie 82740 (the 43 becomes 40).

ii)   82743 – the 4 is less than 5 so the 7 remains the same (seven hundreds) ie 82700 (the 743 becomes 700).

iii)   82743 – the 7 is '5 or more' so the 2 is increased to 3 (three thousands) ie 83000 (the 2743 becomes 3000).

13 Warm-up exercise

Round the numbers to the level of accuracy given:

1   74 to the nearest ten   *Answer* ....

2   125 to the nearest ten   *Answer* ....

3   125 to the nearest hundred   *Answer* ....

4   140086 to the nearest hundred   *Answer* ....

5   140086 to the nearest thousand   *Answer* ....

To what level of accuracy have the numbers been rounded to?

6   7472 is 7500 to the nearest?   *Answer* ....

7   7476 is 7480 to the nearest?   *Answer* ....

8   22084 is 22100 to the nearest?   *Answer* ....

9   22084 is 22000 to the nearest?   *Answer* ....

10   220847 is 220000 to the nearest?   *Answer* ....

14 *Warm-up exercise*

1 Write out two thousand and twenty-two in figures.   *Answer* ....

2 Add 434 and 176.   *Answer* ....

3 Subtract 51 from 246.   *Answer* ....

4 Subtract 2750 from 5342.   *Answer* ....

5 Multiply 9 by 12.   *Answer* ....

6 Multiply 8 × 8.   *Answer* ....

7 Multiply 125 × 45.   *Answer* ....

8 Multiply 1053 × 141.   *Answer* ....

9 Multiply 105 by 100.   *Answer* ....

10 Multiply 25 by 10000.   *Answer* ....

11 Divide 121 by 11.   *Answer* ....

12 Divide 195 by 5.   *Answer* ....

13 Divide 3136 by 14.   *Answer* ....

14 Divide 1728 by 24.   *Answer* ....

15 Divide 1040 by 8.   *Answer* ....

16 $10 + 20 \div 2$ *Answer* ....

17 $20 \div 2 \times 10$ *Answer* ....

18 $10 + 4 - 5 + 7$ *Answer* ....

19 $8 \times 3 \div 4 \times 9$ *Answer* ....

20 $10(5 + 3)$ *Answer* ....

21 $2(8 + 10 \div 2)$ *Answer* ....

22 $3 \times 5(12 \div 3 + 6)$ *Answer* ....

23 Find the factors of 20.   *Answer* ....

24   What are the prime factors of 20?   *Answer* ....

25   Find the factors of 42.   *Answer* ....

26   What are the prime factors of 42?   *Answer* ....

27   Write down the first 6 multiples of 6.   *Answer* ....

28   Write down the first 6 multiples of 9.   *Answer* ....

29   What is the lowest common multiple of 6 and 9?   *Answer* ....

30   What is the lowest common multiple of 20 and 25?   *Answer* ....

31   What is the lowest common multiple of 50 and 250?   *Answer* ....

32   What is the lowest common multiple of 10 and 12?   *Answer* ....

33   540 is 542 rounded to the nearest…   *Answer* ....

34   400 is 435 rounded to the nearest…   *Answer* ....

35   1000 is rounding 1450 to the nearest…   *Answer* ....

Tips for multiplication and division without a calculator

Multiplication

1 To multiply by 4, double the number twice.

2 To multiply by 5, multiply the number by 10 and halve the result.

3 To multiply by 6, multiply the number by 3 and double the result.

4 To multiply by 7 there is no easy method; however, you can multiply the number by 10 then subtract three times the original number.

5 To multiply by 8, double the number three times.

6 To multiply by 9, multiply the number by 10 and then subtract the original number.

7 To multiply by 20, multiply by 10 and then double the result.

8 To multiply by 25, multiply by 100 and divide by 4.

9 To multiply by 50, multiply by 100 and then halve the result.

Division

1 To divide by 4, halve the number and then halve the result.

2 To divide by 5, double the number then divide by 10.

3 To divide by 6, halve the number and divide the result by 3.

4 To divide by 7, there is no easy method.

5 To divide by 8, halve the number, and then halve it twice more.

6 To divide by 9, divide the number by 3 and then by 3 again.

7 To divide by 20, divide by 10 and then halve the result.

8 To divide by 25, divide by 100 and then multiply by 4.

9 To divide by 50, divide by 100 and then halve the result.

Understanding fractions

We use fractions in everyday situations; for example, we talk about *half* an hour, *three-quarters* of a mile and *one-third* off the price. Despite these everyday uses, some people have difficulty with the concept of fractions and find problems involving fractions extremely difficult. One way to explain fractions is to say that the whole is divided into a number of *equal parts*, where we have one or more parts.

All fractions have a top and a bottom number. The bottom number, or *denominator*, tells us how many equal parts the whole is divided into. The top number, or *numerator*, tells us how many parts we have. So half an hour means that we *divide* the hour into two equal parts and we have one part.

Another way to understand fractions is to draw the whole, divide it up into equal parts and shade in the fraction. One-quarter is:

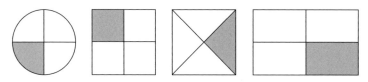

Similarly, the fraction three-quarters can be shown as:

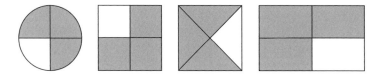

The above diagrams show how one-quarter added to three-quarters completes the whole.

An alternative way of looking at a fraction is to consider it as a division, where the horizontal bar separating the top and bottom numbers means divided by, for example:

$\dfrac{1}{2} = 1 \div 2$; (half = one whole divided by two)

$\dfrac{3}{4} = 3 \div 4$; (three quarters = three wholes divided by four)

$\dfrac{1}{3} = 1 \div 3$ (one third = one whole divided by three)

Diagrams can be used to explain the division process. If four people *share equally* three pizzas they will receive three-quarters of a pizza each, which can be shown as follows:

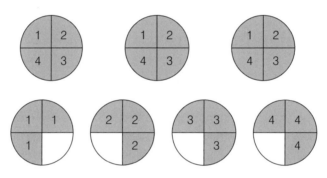

So three pizzas divided equally between four people is 3 ÷ 4 each, or three-quarters per person. Looking at the individual quarters we can see that there are twelve quarters in total and twelve quarters divided amongst four people is three quarters each.

When comparing the sizes of fractions with the *same denominator*, the largest fraction has the largest numerator so

$\dfrac{3}{4}$ is greater than $\dfrac{2}{4}$ which is greater than $\dfrac{1}{4}$

Cancelling (equivalent fractions)

Some fractions can be cancelled so as to express them in smaller numbers. The value of the fraction is *not altered by cancelling* and so is an '*equivalent fraction*'.

For example, *four-sixths* can be expressed as a fraction having smaller numbers, by dividing *both* the top and bottom numbers by 2. This is known as *cancelling*.

$\dfrac{4^{\div 2}}{6^{\div 2}} = \dfrac{2}{3}$

Remember, the value of the fraction has not become smaller, only the numbers involved – this means that *four-sixths* and *two-thirds* are equivalent fractions:

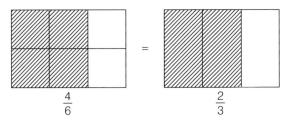

$$\frac{4}{6} \qquad = \qquad \frac{2}{3}$$

Another example of cancelling is $\frac{8}{16}$. This fraction can be cancelled three times as follows:

$\frac{8}{16}$ can be cancelled to $\frac{4}{8}$ by dividing the 8 and the 16 by 2

$\frac{8}{16}$ can be cancelled to $\frac{2}{4}$ by dividing the 8 and the 16 by 4

$\frac{8}{16}$ can be cancelled to $\frac{1}{2}$ by dividing the 8 and the 16 by 8

So the equivalent fractions are $\frac{8}{16} = \frac{4}{8} = \frac{2}{4} = \frac{1}{2}$

If we cancel $\frac{8}{16}$ to $\frac{1}{2}$, this is known as cancelling a fraction to its lowest terms (it cannot be reduced any further):

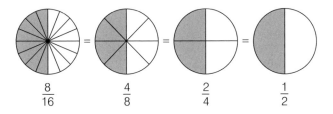

$$\frac{8}{16} \qquad \frac{4}{8} \qquad \frac{2}{4} \qquad \frac{1}{2}$$

When comparing the sizes of fractions with the *same numerator* we can see that the largest fraction has the smallest denominator:

$\frac{1}{2}$ is greater than $\frac{1}{4}$ which is greater than $\frac{1}{8}$ which is greater than $\frac{1}{16}$

15 *Warm-up exercise*

Cancel the following fractions to their lowest terms (use factors):

1 $\dfrac{3}{6}$ (divide the top and the bottom by 3)   *Answer* ....

2 $\dfrac{15}{20}$ (divide the top and the bottom by 5)   *Answer* ....

3 $\dfrac{12}{36}$ (divide top and bottom by 12, or by 3 and
then by 4)   *Answer* ....

4 $\dfrac{40}{72}$ (divide top and bottom by 2, three times over)   *Answer* ....

5 $\dfrac{16}{24}$ (try dividing by small numbers like 2, 3 or 4)   *Answer* ....

6 $\dfrac{18}{30}$ (try dividing by 2 and then 3)   *Answer* ....

7 $\dfrac{10}{100}$ (numbers ending in zero always divide by 10)   *Answer* ....

8 $\dfrac{95}{100}$ (numbers ending in 5 always divide by 5)   *Answer* ....

9 $\dfrac{8}{12}$ (use the methods outlined earlier for factors
and primes)   *Answer* ....

10 $\dfrac{40}{100}$ (use the methods outlined for factors
and primes)   *Answer* ....

Addition and subtraction of fractions

Addition and subtraction of fractions can be dealt with together as the same 'rules' apply to both. Multiplication and division of fractions have different rules and will be explained separately. To be able to add or subtract fractions they must have the same denominators. Take the following example:

$$\frac{1}{8} + \frac{3}{8}$$

Both fractions have a denominator of 8. We write the denominator *once*, and then add the two top numbers:

$$\text{so } \frac{1}{8} + \frac{3}{8} = \frac{1+3}{8} = \frac{4}{8}$$

An example of subtraction is:

$$\frac{13}{16} - \frac{5}{16} = \frac{13-5}{16} = \frac{8}{16}$$

16 *Warm-up exercise*

Add/subtract the following fractions then cancel where possible:

1 $\dfrac{6}{8} + \dfrac{1}{8}$ *Answer* ....

2 $\dfrac{2}{6} + \dfrac{3}{6}$ *Answer* ....

3 $\dfrac{7}{10} + \dfrac{4}{10}$ *Answer* ....

4 $\dfrac{11}{12} + \dfrac{4}{12}$ *Answer* ....

5 $\dfrac{7}{9} - \dfrac{2}{9} + \dfrac{4}{9}$ *Answer* ....

6 $\dfrac{11}{12} - \dfrac{5}{12}$ *Answer* ....

7 $\dfrac{9}{15} + \dfrac{1}{15}$ *Answer* ....

8 $\dfrac{12}{40} - \dfrac{4}{40}$ *Answer* ....

When the fractions have different denominators we can still add or subtract them, but in order to do so we first of all have to find a *common denominator*, ie a number which both denominators will divide into. Take the following example:

$$\frac{1}{4} + \frac{3}{6}$$

The first fraction has a denominator of 4 and the second fraction has a denominator of 6. The *common denominator* is a number which both 4 and 6 will divide into. There are many numbers which both 4 and 6 will divide into. To find them we compare the four times table with six times table and see where they give us the same answer. From these tables, we can see that 4 and 6 have common denominators at 12, 24, 36 and 48. To make the working easier we choose the *lowest* of these – 12.

Four times table	Six times table
$1 \times 4 = 4$	$1 \times 6 = 6$
$2 \times 4 = 8$	$2 \times 6 = \underline{\mathbf{12}}$
$3 \times 4 = \underline{\mathbf{12}}$	$3 \times 6 = 18$
$4 \times 4 = 16$	$4 \times 6 = \underline{\mathbf{24}}$
$5 \times 4 = 20$	$5 \times 6 = 30$
$6 \times 4 = \underline{\mathbf{24}}$	$6 \times 6 = \underline{\mathbf{36}}$
$7 \times 4 = 28$	$7 \times 6 = 42$
$8 \times 4 = 32$	$8 \times 6 = \underline{\mathbf{48}}$
$9 \times 4 = \underline{\mathbf{36}}$	$9 \times 6 = 54$
$10 \times 4 = 40$	$10 \times 6 = 60$
$11 \times 4 = 44$	$11 \times 6 = 66$
$12 \times 4 = \underline{\mathbf{48}}$	$12 \times 6 = 72$

The tables show us that 12 is the lowest common denominator (LCD). To proceed with the sum, the next stage is to rewrite each fraction in terms of the common denominator, ie twelfths. So we re-write $\frac{1}{4}$ in twelfths and $\frac{3}{6}$ in twelfths.

To do this we divide the common denominator 12 by the denominators of the two fractions (4 and 6 in the above example) and then multiply the numerator of each fraction by the respective answer.

We rewrite $\frac{1}{4}$ in twelfths as follows:

$12 \div 4 = 3$ (common denominator 12 ÷ denominator of 4 = **3**)

$\mathbf{3} \times 1 = 3$ (answer 3 × numerator of 1 = 3)

So we have: $\frac{1}{4} = \frac{3}{12}$

Similarly $\dfrac{3}{6}$ in twelfths is rewritten:

$12 \div 6 = 2$ (common denominator $12 \div$ denominator of $6 = $ **2**)

2 $\times 3 = 6$ (answer $2 \times$ numerator of $3 = 6$)

So we have: $\dfrac{3}{6} = \dfrac{6}{12}$

The sum of $\dfrac{1}{4} + \dfrac{3}{6}$ now becomes: $\dfrac{3}{12} + \dfrac{6}{12} = \dfrac{9}{12}$

Subtraction of fractions with different denominators is carried out in exactly the same way.

Note that two (or more) numbers, even prime numbers, *always* have a common denominator. If we take any two numbers, for example 3 and 13, we can multiply them to find a common denominator: $3 \times 13 = 39$. The 3 goes into 39 thirteen times and the 13 goes into 39 three times, so 3 and 13 have 39 as a common denominator. When adding one-quarter and three-sixths in an earlier example we could have multiplied the denominators of 4 and 6 to give 24 and then worked in 24ths rather than in 12ths (the LCD). You can work with any common denominator but the LCD makes the numerators smaller and easier to work with, and the answer requires less cancelling. For example, 20ths and 25ths have a denominator of $20 \times 25 = 500$, but the LCD is only 100.

$\dfrac{1}{20} + \dfrac{1}{25} = \dfrac{25}{500} + \dfrac{20}{500} = \dfrac{45}{500} = \dfrac{9}{100}$ (using the LCD of 500)

$\dfrac{1}{20} + \dfrac{1}{25} = \dfrac{5}{100} + \dfrac{4}{100} = \dfrac{9}{100}$ (using the LCD of 100)

Note that if one denominator divides into the other denominator exactly then the larger denominator is the LCD of both denominators. For example, the denominators 2 and 12 have an LCD of 12 (because 2 divides into 12 six times and 12 divides into 12 once; 12 is the lowest number that 12 divides into exactly). So always check to see if the lowest denominator divides into the highest denominator when adding or subtracting fractions; if it does then you have the LCD straight away.

17 *Warm-up exercise*

Work out the *lowest common denominator* (LCD) only:

1 $\dfrac{1}{5}$ and $\dfrac{4}{15}$ *Answer* ....

2 $\dfrac{1}{4}$ and $\dfrac{2}{3}$ *Answer* ....

3 $\dfrac{13}{16}$ and $\dfrac{1}{8}$ and $\dfrac{3}{4}$ *Answer* ....

Calculate the following using the LCDs above:

4 $\dfrac{1}{5} + \dfrac{4}{15}$ *Answer* ....

5 $\dfrac{1}{4} + \dfrac{2}{3}$ *Answer* ....

6 $\dfrac{13}{16} + \dfrac{1}{8} - \dfrac{3}{4}$ *Answer* ....

18 *Warm-up exercise*

Work out the LCD and then *choose the largest fraction*. Try to work out the answers 'in your head' as far as possible:

1 $\dfrac{2}{3}$ and $\dfrac{3}{4}$ *Answer* ....

2 $\dfrac{2}{3}$ and $\dfrac{5}{9}$ and $\dfrac{11}{18}$ *Answer* ....

3 $\dfrac{1}{3}$ and $\dfrac{2}{5}$ and $\dfrac{11}{30}$ *Answer* ....

4 $\dfrac{5}{6}$ and $\dfrac{3}{4}$ and $\dfrac{7}{8}$ *Answer* ....

5 $\dfrac{30}{100}$ and $\dfrac{7}{25}$ and $\dfrac{16}{50}$ *Answer* ....

6 $\dfrac{75}{1000}$ and $\dfrac{7}{100}$ and $\dfrac{3}{50}$ *Answer* ....

Multiplication and division of fractions

Multiplication is straightforward. All you have to do is multiply the two numerators (top numbers) together and multiply the two denominators (bottom numbers) together. For example:

$$\text{eg } \frac{1}{5} \times \frac{2}{3} = \frac{1 \times 2}{5 \times 3} = \frac{2}{15}$$

So when multiplying fractions together the rule is:

$$\frac{\textit{Multiply the two top numbers}}{\textit{Multiply the two bottom numbers}}$$

The answer is always smaller than either of the original fractions and always between 0 and 1.

19 Warm-up exercise

Calculate the following and cancel the answer where possible:

1 $\frac{2}{3} \times \frac{1}{9}$ *Answer* ....

6 $\frac{2}{3} \times \frac{3}{4}$ *Answer* ....

2 $\frac{4}{15} \times \frac{2}{3}$ *Answer* ....

7 $\frac{3}{5} \times \frac{5}{9}$ *Answer* ....

3 $\frac{4}{7} \times \frac{4}{9}$ *Answer* ....

8 $\frac{7}{20} \times \frac{5}{7}$ *Answer* ....

4 $\frac{2}{3} \times \frac{1}{9}$ *Answer* ....

9 $\frac{2}{9} \times \frac{3}{9}$ *Answer* ....

5 $\frac{3}{5} \times \frac{1}{100}$ *Answer* ....

10 $\frac{9}{10} \times \frac{1}{3}$ *Answer* ....

Division of fractions is similar except the fraction on the right-hand side must be:

(i) turned upside down (eg $\frac{3}{5}$ becomes $\frac{5}{3}$)

(ii) then multiplied with the fraction on the left-hand side eg $\frac{1}{5} \div \frac{3}{10} = ?$

Stage (i) $\dfrac{3}{10}$ becomes $\dfrac{10}{3}$

Stage (ii) $\dfrac{1}{5} \times \dfrac{10}{3} = \dfrac{10}{15}$

So when dividing fractions the rule is:

Turn the right-hand fraction upside down and then multiply the two fractions together. This can be explained as follows: if we take 6 and multiply it by one-twelfth we have six-twelfths, but if we take 6 wholes and divide them into twelfths we have $6 \times 12 = 72$:

$$\text{So } 6 \times \dfrac{1}{12} = \dfrac{6}{12} \text{ but } 6 \div \dfrac{1}{12} = 72 \ (6 \times \dfrac{12}{1} = 72)$$

We can see that any number divided by a fraction gives a larger number.

20 Warm-up exercise

Calculate the following divisions by turning the right-hand-side fraction upside down and *multiplying by it*:

1 $\quad \dfrac{1}{6} \div \dfrac{1}{4} \qquad$ *Answer* ....

6 $\quad \dfrac{12}{100} \div \dfrac{3}{10} \qquad$ *Answer* ....

2 $\quad \dfrac{1}{3} \div \dfrac{5}{9} \qquad$ *Answer* ....

7 $\quad \dfrac{8}{1000} \div \dfrac{1}{5} \qquad$ *Answer* ....

3 $\quad \dfrac{3}{16} \div \dfrac{1}{4} \qquad$ *Answer* ....

8 $\quad \dfrac{1}{250} \div \dfrac{4}{5} \qquad$ *Answer* ....

4 $\quad \dfrac{3}{10} \div \dfrac{3}{5} \qquad$ *Answer* ....

9 $\quad \dfrac{2}{125} \div \dfrac{8}{75} \qquad$ *Answer* ....

5 $\quad \dfrac{5}{12} \div \dfrac{1}{2} \qquad$ *Answer* ....

10 $\quad \dfrac{3}{7} \div \dfrac{9}{14} \qquad$ *Answer* ....

Improper fractions

Until now, we have worked with fractions that have denominators greater than the numerator (bottom greater than top). For example:

$\dfrac{1}{4}, \dfrac{5}{6}, \dfrac{9}{10}, \dfrac{13}{16}$ – these are known as 'vulgar fractions'.

However, some fractions are *top heavy*, eg $\dfrac{17}{6}, \dfrac{9}{4}, \dfrac{65}{25}$ – the numerator is greater than the denominator. These fractions are known as 'improper fractions', and are added, subtracted, multiplied and divided in the same way as for vulgar fractions. For example:

$$\frac{5}{2} + \frac{7}{3} = \frac{15 + 14}{6} = \frac{29}{6}$$

$$\frac{9}{5} - \frac{10}{7} = \frac{63 - 50}{35} = \frac{13}{35}$$

$$\frac{9}{4} \times \frac{8}{5} = \frac{72}{20} = \frac{18}{5}$$

$$\frac{11}{4} \div \frac{9}{7} = \frac{11}{4} \times \frac{7}{9} = \frac{77}{36}$$

21 Warm-up exercise

Work out the following sums containing improper fractions, and cancel your answers where possible:

1 $\dfrac{7}{6} + \dfrac{11}{12}$ *Answer* ....

5 $\dfrac{12}{5} + \dfrac{5}{2}$ *Answer* ....

2 $\dfrac{14}{3} - \dfrac{9}{2}$ *Answer* ....

6 $\dfrac{5}{3} \times \dfrac{8}{5}$ *Answer* ....

3 $\dfrac{5}{4} \times \dfrac{3}{2}$ *Answer* ....

7 $\dfrac{25}{6} \div \dfrac{15}{8}$ *Answer* ....

4 $\dfrac{6}{5} \div \dfrac{12}{5}$ *Answer* ....

8 $\dfrac{75}{20} \times \dfrac{40}{3}$ *Answer* ....

Mixed fractions (or mixed numbers)

A mixed fraction consists of a whole number with a vulgar fraction. Examples of mixed fractions are:

$$1\frac{1}{2}, \ 2\frac{5}{6}, \ 5\frac{1}{3}, \ 3\frac{3}{4}$$

To be able to work out the problems containing mixed fractions we have to turn the mixed fraction into an improper fraction. To do this, we first separate the whole number from the *vulgar* fraction; for example:

$$1\frac{1}{2} \text{ is 1 whole and 1 half: } 1 + \frac{1}{2}$$

The next step is to write the whole number in terms of the fraction. In the above example, 1 is 2 halves, so

$$1 = \frac{2}{2}$$

We can now add the whole, expressed as a fraction, to the vulgar fraction:

$$1\frac{1}{2} = \frac{2}{2} + \frac{1}{2} = \frac{3}{2}$$

so $1\frac{1}{2}$ as an improper fraction is $\frac{3}{2}$.

Similarly, $2\frac{3}{4} = \frac{8}{4} + \frac{3}{4} = \frac{11}{4}$

This example can also be shown in diagram form:

A more mathematical way of converting a mixed fraction to an improper fraction is as follows:

Step (i)   Multiply the whole number by the denominator of the vulgar fraction.

Step (ii)   Put the answer in step (i) over the denominator of the vulgar fraction.

Step (iii) Combine the vulgar fraction with the answer in step (ii).

For example, express the mixed fraction $2\frac{1}{4}$ as an improper fraction:

Step (i) $2 \times 4 = 8$

Step (ii) $\frac{8}{4}$ (2 wholes = 8 quarters)

Step (iii) $\frac{8}{4} + \frac{1}{4} = \frac{9}{4}$

So $2\frac{1}{4}$ as an improper fraction is $\frac{9}{4}$.

22 *Warm-up exercise*

Convert the following mixed fractions to improper fractions and cancel where possible:

1 $1\frac{3}{4}$ *Answer* ....

6 $1\frac{19}{100}$ *Answer* ....

2 $5\frac{1}{2}$ *Answer* ....

7 $1\frac{20}{100}$ *Answer* ....

3 $2\frac{5}{6}$ *Answer* ....

8 $2\frac{10}{25}$ *Answer* ....

4 $3\frac{3}{8}$ *Answer* ....

9 $1\frac{400}{1000}$ *Answer* ....

5 $6\frac{7}{10}$ *Answer* ....

It is also possible to convert an improper fraction into a mixed fraction – the reverse of above. For example:

$\frac{27}{8}, \frac{9}{1}, \frac{7}{3}, \frac{11}{10},$ can be converted to mixed fractions.

This is done as follows:

Step (i)   Divide the numerator by the denominator.

Step (ii)   Put the remainder (from the answer in step (i)) over the denominator of the improper fraction.

Step (iii)   Combine the whole number (from the answer in step (i)) with the answer in step (ii).

For example, express the improper fraction $\dfrac{21}{4}$ as a mixed fraction.

Step (i) $\quad 4\overline{)21}$ with 5 remainder $\mathbf{1}$

Step (ii) $\quad \dfrac{1}{4}$

Step (iii) combine 5 with $\dfrac{1}{4}$ to give $5\dfrac{1}{4}$

so $\dfrac{21}{4} = 5\dfrac{1}{4}$

23 Warm-up exercise

Convert the following improper fractions to mixed fractions:

1 $\dfrac{9}{2}$ *Answer* ....

2 $\dfrac{23}{4}$ *Answer* ....

3 $\dfrac{16}{3}$ *Answer* ....

4 $\dfrac{50}{3}$ *Answer* ....

5 $\dfrac{42}{8}$ *Answer* ....

6 $\dfrac{125}{10}$ *Answer* ....

Multiplication and division of fractions by whole numbers

Here it is helpful to rewrite the whole number as an *improper fraction with a denominator of 1*, before carrying out the calculation.

For example, 2, 3, 4, 5 etc can be rewritten as $\dfrac{2}{1}, \dfrac{3}{1}, \dfrac{4}{1}, \dfrac{5}{1}$:

$$\frac{5}{6} \times 2 = \frac{5}{6} \times \frac{2}{1} = \frac{10}{6} = 1\frac{4}{6} = 1\frac{2}{3}$$

$$\frac{5}{6} \times 3 = \frac{5}{6} \times \frac{3}{1} = \frac{15}{6} = 2\frac{3}{6} = 2\frac{1}{2}$$

$$\frac{5}{6} \times 4 = \frac{5}{6} \times \frac{4}{1} = \frac{20}{6} = 3\frac{2}{6} = 3\frac{1}{3}$$

$$\frac{5}{6} \times 5 = \frac{5}{6} \times \frac{5}{1} = \frac{25}{6} = 4\frac{1}{6}$$

24 Warm-up exercise

Multiply or divide the following fractions by the whole numbers shown and express your answers as mixed fractions:

1 $\dfrac{1}{2} \times 5$ *Answer* ....   **5** $\dfrac{50}{80} \times 12$ *Answer* ....

2 $\dfrac{3}{4} \times 6$ *Answer* ....   **6** $\dfrac{3}{4} \div 5$ *Answer* ....

3 $\dfrac{7}{8} \times 4$ *Answer* ....   **7** $\dfrac{4}{9} \div 16$ *Answer* ....

4 $\dfrac{9}{5} \times 6$ *Answer* ....   **8** $\dfrac{5}{6} \div 20$ *Answer* ....

How to cross-cancel fractions

Often you can avoid large numbers in calculations by cancelling fractions *diagonally* rather than just top and bottom. Cross-cancelling helps to *simplify* the arithmetic. For example:

$\dfrac{7}{8} \times \dfrac{9}{14}$ Without cross-cancelling this becomes $\dfrac{63}{112}$

In cross-cancelling, the 7 can be cancelled diagonally with the 14 ('7 goes into 7 once and 7 goes into 14 twice'). The calculation then becomes $\dfrac{1}{8} \times \dfrac{9}{2}$ giving $\dfrac{9}{16}$ as the answer. For example:

$\dfrac{8}{15} \times \dfrac{5}{16}$ Without cross-cancelling this becomes $\dfrac{40}{240}$

In cross-cancelling, the 8 can be cancelled diagonally with the 16, and the 5 can be cancelled diagonally with the 15. The calculation becomes $\dfrac{1}{3} \times \dfrac{1}{2}$ giving $\dfrac{1}{6}$ as the answer.

It is difficult to cross-cancel 'in your head' so you would normally write the calculation as follows:

$$\frac{\overset{1}{\cancel{8}}}{\underset{3}{\cancel{15}}} \times \frac{\overset{1}{\cancel{5}}}{\underset{2}{\cancel{16}}} = \frac{1}{3} \times \frac{1}{2} = \frac{1}{6}$$

25 *Warm-up exercise*

Work out the following by cross-cancelling as a first step. Express your answers as mixed fractions or whole numbers:

1 $\dfrac{7}{3} \times \dfrac{3}{5}$ *Answer* ....   **4** $\dfrac{3}{10} \times 100$ *Answer* ....

2 $\dfrac{51}{16} \times \dfrac{4}{3}$ *Answer* ....   **5** $\dfrac{32}{40} \times 80$ *Answer* ....

3 $\dfrac{240}{50} \times \dfrac{5}{3}$ *Answer* ....   **6** $\dfrac{36}{500} \times 1000$ *Answer* ....

(In the following divisions, cross-cancel *after* turning the right-hand-side number upside down.)

7 $\dfrac{5}{12} \div \dfrac{16}{24}$ *Answer* ....   **12** $\dfrac{14}{216} \div \dfrac{28}{36}$ *Answer* ....

8 $\dfrac{17}{100} \div \dfrac{34}{50}$ *Answer* ....   **13** $\dfrac{3}{4} \div \dfrac{375}{1000}$ *Answer* ....

9 $\dfrac{27}{100} \div \dfrac{3}{5}$ *Answer* ....   **14** $\dfrac{48}{60} \div \dfrac{80}{360}$ *Answer* ....

10 $\dfrac{40}{150} \div \dfrac{64}{120}$ *Answer* ....   **15** $\dfrac{15}{100} \div 60$ *Answer* ....

11 $\dfrac{30}{144} \div \dfrac{110}{132}$ *Answer* ....

26 *Warm-up exercise*

Work out the following by first converting the mixed fractions to improper fractions. The answers are all whole numbers:

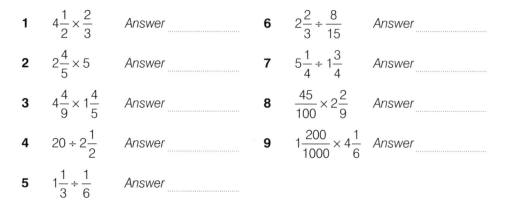

1 $4\dfrac{1}{2} \times \dfrac{2}{3}$ *Answer* ....   **6** $2\dfrac{2}{3} \div \dfrac{8}{15}$ *Answer* ....

2 $2\dfrac{4}{5} \times 5$ *Answer* ....   **7** $5\dfrac{1}{4} \div 1\dfrac{3}{4}$ *Answer* ....

3 $4\dfrac{4}{9} \times 1\dfrac{4}{5}$ *Answer* ....   **8** $\dfrac{45}{100} \times 2\dfrac{2}{9}$ *Answer* ....

4 $20 \div 2\dfrac{1}{2}$ *Answer* ....   **9** $1\dfrac{200}{1000} \times 4\dfrac{1}{6}$ *Answer* ....

5 $1\dfrac{1}{3} \div \dfrac{1}{6}$ *Answer* ....

Ratios and proportional parts

Ratios are similar to fractions and they show you how a whole is divided into parts. Examples of ratios are 5:2 (five parts to two parts), 3:1 (three parts to one part), 1:4 (one part to four parts), 3:2:6 (three parts to two parts to six parts). The ratio tells you how many parts in total are present in the whole.

Example: a ratio of 5:2 means there are 7 parts in the whole (5 + 2). A ratio of 3:2:6 means there are 11 parts in the whole (3 + 2 + 6).

So for a ratio of 5:2 the whole is split into sevenths, and for a ratio of 3:2:6 the whole is split into elevenths. To find out how much each part of the ratio is of the whole we divide each part by the total number of parts.

So, 5:2 means that the whole is divided into $\frac{5}{7}$ and $\frac{2}{7}$

A ratio of 3:2:6 means that the whole is divided into $\frac{3}{11}$, $\frac{2}{11}$ and $\frac{6}{11}$

This is known as dividing a quantity into proportional parts.

For example: divide 60 in the ratio 3:1.

First step: Work out the number of parts in the whole, in this case: 3 + 1 = 4 (four quarters).

Second step: Work out the proportional parts (the fractions), these are $\frac{3}{4}$ and $\frac{1}{4}$.

Third step: Multiply the whole by the proportional parts: $\frac{3}{4} \times 60 = 45$; and $\frac{1}{4} \times 60 = 15$

So 60 in the ratio 3:1 is 45:15.

The proportional parts when added together give the whole:

45 + 15 = 60

Ratios can be simplified in a similar way to fractions by cancelling *both sides* by a common factor (eg by 2, by 3 etc).

Example: The ratio of boys to girls in a science class of 28 is 16:12. Express this ratio in its simplest terms.

16:12 = 8:6 = 4:3 ie there are 4 boys for every 3 girls

Example: the ratio of boys to girls in a class of 25 is 40:60. How many boys are there and how many girls are there? We can simplify this ratio by looking for common factors (numbers to divide by), in this example 10 and 2:

$40 \div 10 = 4$; $60 \div 10 = 6$;

so $40:60 = 4:6$, which reduces to $2:3$ if we divide both sides by 2.

A ratio of 2:3 means that there are 5 parts in the whole $(2 + 3)$ and the whole is split into two-fifths boys (2 parts) and three-fifths girls (3 parts).

$$\text{boys} = \frac{2}{5} \times 25 = 2 \times 5 = 10 \text{ boys}$$

girls = total − boys = 25 − 10 = 15 girls (subtracting boys from the total is quicker than multiplying 25 by the fraction of girls)

Note that ratio of 40:60 does not mean that there are 100 pupils. There can be any number of pupils, fewer or more than 100. The lowest possible number of pupils is 5 (2 boys and 3 girls). Like a percentage, a ratio is just another way of expressing a fraction.

The method is the same when there are three terms. For example:

The ratio of girls to boys to teachers on a school trip is 5:4:1. Determine the number of girls, boys and teachers if 40 people went on the trip.

Method:

i)   Work out the total number of parts.

ii) Work out the proportional parts (fractions).

iii) Multiply the proportional parts by the whole.

First step: Number of parts = 5 + 4 + 1 = 10

Second step: Work out the proportional parts:

$$\frac{5}{10}; \frac{4}{10}; \frac{1}{10}$$

Third step: Multiply the whole by the proportional parts:

$$\frac{5}{10} \times 40 = 20 \text{ girls}; \frac{4}{10} \times 40 = 16 \text{ boys}; \frac{1}{10} \times 40 = 4 \text{ teachers}$$

In all three answers you are multiplying by 40 and dividing by 10, which is the same as multiplying by 4. In other words, there are 4 'people per part'. So instead of using fractions you can multiply the ratio 5:4:1 by 4 to give 20:16:4, which are the respective numbers of girls, boys and teachers.

In another type of ratio question, the total number in one of the proportions is given rather than the total number in the whole.

Example: if the ratio of boys to girl in a class is 5:4 and there are 20 boys, how many girls are in the class?

Here, we are not given the total number of pupils in the class, only the *number of boys*.

We have 5 parts equal to 20 boys, or $\frac{5}{9}$ class = 20

There are a few ways to tackle this problem; two non-algebra methods are explained.

i) Intuitive fractions method

We are asked to find the number of girls. We can see that the answer will be less than 20 because the number of girls equals 4 parts (boys are 5 parts). For every 5 boys there are 4 girls, so for every 1 boy there must be 4 ÷ 5, or 4/5 girl.

We have 20 boys so we must have $20 \times \frac{4}{5} = 4 \times 4 = 16$ girls.

ii) One-part first method

We have 5 parts equal to 20 boys. We can work out one-part by dividing five-parts by 5. Then we multiply one-part by 4 to give the number of girls (4 parts).

5 parts class = 20, so 1 part class = 20 ÷ 5 = 4 (one-ninth of the class = 4);
Girls = 4 parts = 4 × 4 = 16.

27 *Warm-up exercise*

1   Divide 60p in the ratio of 5:1   *Answer* ....

2   Divide £30 in the ratio of 2:3   *Answer* ....

3   Divide 125 in the ratio of 19:6   *Answer* ....

4   Divide 600 in the ratio of 3:2:1   *Answer* ....

5   Divide 250 in the ratio of 5:4:1   *Answer* ....

28 *Warm-up exercise*

1   Place the following fractions in order of size starting
with the smallest fraction:

$$\frac{5}{20} \quad \frac{2}{20} \quad \frac{19}{20} \quad \frac{11}{20}$$

Answer ....

2   Place the following fractions in order of size
starting with the smallest fraction:

$$\frac{5}{20} \quad \frac{5}{10} \quad \frac{5}{25} \quad \frac{5}{125}$$

Answer ....

3   Find the two equivalent fractions $\frac{2}{3}, \frac{3}{5}, \frac{6}{9}, \frac{8}{10}$

Answer ....

4   Place the following fractions in order of size
starting with the smallest fraction:

$$\frac{5}{10} \quad \frac{11}{20} \quad \frac{1}{5} \quad \frac{12}{40}$$

Answer ....

5   What is the missing numerator? $\frac{6}{10} = \frac{?}{5}$

Answer ....

6   What is the missing denominator? $\frac{2}{3} = \frac{8}{?}$

Answer ....

7   Reduce the fraction $\frac{5}{25}$ to its lowest terms.

Answer ....

8   Cancel the fraction $\frac{36}{60}$ to its lowest terms.

Answer ....

9   Reduce $\frac{15}{90}$ to its lowest terms.

Answer ....

10   Cancel $\frac{35}{100}$

Answer ....

11   Add $\frac{3}{6}$ and $\frac{2}{6}$

Answer ....

12 $\frac{1}{5} + \frac{2}{5}$

Answer ....

13   Subtract $\frac{5}{8}$ from $\frac{7}{8}$ and simplify your answer.

Answer ....

14 $\dfrac{5}{9} - \dfrac{3}{9}$

Answer ....

15 $\dfrac{5}{32} - \dfrac{1}{8}$

Answer ....

16   Simplify $\dfrac{3}{4} - \dfrac{2}{3}$

Answer ....

17 $\dfrac{3}{4} \times \dfrac{1}{2}$

Answer ....

18   What is $\dfrac{2}{3} \times \dfrac{1}{4}$ in its lowest terms?

Answer ....

19 $\dfrac{3}{10} \div 6$

Answer ....

20   What is $\dfrac{1}{4}$ of 24?

Answer ....

21   20 seconds are what fraction of 1 minute?

Answer ....

22   Convert $\dfrac{27}{7}$ to a mixed fraction.

Answer ....

23   Convert $4\dfrac{1}{2}$ to an improper fraction.

Answer ....

24   Write $\dfrac{18}{6}$ in its lowest terms.

Answer ....

25   Write $\dfrac{10}{4}$ in its lowest terms.

Answer ....

26   Multiply $\dfrac{1}{3}$ by 120

Answer ....

27   What is $\dfrac{2}{3}$ of 75?

Answer ....

28 $\dfrac{7}{8} \times 7$

Answer ....

29   Solve $\dfrac{33}{7} - 4$

Answer ....

30 $\dfrac{2}{7} \div \dfrac{2}{5}$

Answer ....

31   Divide 36 in the ratio 5:7   *Answer* ....

32   In a Maths class of 24 pupils the ratio of pupils
         at Key Stage 5 to Key Stage 6 in Maths is 7:5.
         How many pupils are at Key Stage 5?   *Answer* ....

33   If the ratio of boys to girls in a class is 7:9 and
         there are 32 pupils, find:

         i) the number of boys;   *Answer* ....

         ii) the number of girls.   *Answer* ....

Understanding decimals

Decimal numbers are numbers that contain a decimal point (d.p.). Decimal fractions are decimal numbers smaller than one (nought point something); they are fractions of a whole number. The decimal point (.) separates the whole number from the decimal fraction.

Decimal in words	Decimal in figures			
	Units	Tenths	Hun.ths	Thou.ths
three point five eight	3.	5	8	
one point two five six	1.	2	5	6
nought point seven three	0.	7	3	

Note: in a decimal fraction, pronounce each numeral separately. So for 0.73 in the last line above, say *nought point seven three* not nought point seventy-three.

Necessary and unnecessary zeros

It is important to understand which zeros are needed and which are not when writing both whole numbers and decimals. Whole numbers such as 2, 10 and 250 should not be written as 2.0, 10.0 and 250.0 – the decimal point and nought after it are unnecessary and could lead to errors if misread as 20, 100 and 2500. For a similar reason, a zero should always be placed in front of the decimal point when there is no other number (eg write 0.73 not .73).

The following are examples of unnecessary zeros:

0.30   0.300   0.3000   which should all be written as 0.3
0.850   0.8500   0.85000   which should be written as 0.85

The following are examples of necessary zeros:

0.3   0.03   0.003   which all have different values
0.802   0.8002   0.80002   which all have different values

29 *Warm-up exercise*

Write out the following numbers in figures:

1	Twenty two point five	*Answer* ....
2	Nought point two seven five	*Answer* ....
3	Nought point nought two	*Answer* ....
4	Two hundred point zero seven five	*Answer* ....
5	One hundred and two point three seven five	*Answer* ....

30 *Warm-up exercise*

In each of the five questions below place the four numbers in order of size, starting with the smallest number and ending with the largest.

	(a)	(b)	(c)	(d)
1	2.5	0.25	0.3	0.025
2	0.05	0.1	0.08	0.075
3	3.025	3.25	3.05	3.04
4	6.20	6.02	6.026	6.22
5	10.01	10.101	10.011	10.11

Multiplication by powers of ten (×10, ×100, ×1000)

To multiply a decimal number by 10, 100, 1000 etc, you just move the decimal point (d.p.) to the *right* by however many *powers of ten* you have – or put another way, by how many noughts you have (a calculator is not required). To multiply:

  × 10 you move the decimal point (d.p.) 1 place to the right
  × 100 you move the d.p. 2 places to the right
  × 1000 you move the d.p. 3 places to the right

For example, what is 5.178×100?

    answer: $5.178 \times 100 = 517.8$
    similarly: $0.0235 \times 10 = 0.235$

Division by powers of ten (÷10, ÷100, ÷1000)

Just as in the multiplication of decimals, you can divide decimals by powers of ten (10, 100, 1000, etc) by moving the decimal point. This is simply the reverse of the multiplication case so when dividing you move the decimal point to the *left*. For example:

    25.34 ÷ 10   = 2.534
           ÷ 100   = 0.2534
           ÷ 1000 = 0.02534

Other examples are:

    256.98 ÷ 100 = 2.5698
           ÷ 1000 = 0.25698

Similarly: $0.0037 \div 100 = 0.000037$

31 Warm-up exercise

Work out the following multiplications and divisions. Hint: the number of zeros following the 1 is the number of places to move the decimal point – either to the right (to multiply) or to the left (to divide):

1 1.5897×1000 *Answer* ....

2 $7692105 \div 10000$ *Answer* ....

3 31.729×100 *Answer* ....

4 $0.175 \div 10$ *Answer* ....

5 17.1703×1000 *Answer* ....

6 0.025×1000 *Answer* ....

7 0.0058×1000 *Answer* ....

8 0.0001×1000000 *Answer* ....

Addition, subtraction, multiplication and division of decimals

The addition and subtraction of decimal numbers is the same as for ordinary numbers. The only thing to remember is to keep the decimal points aligned; adding unnecessary zeros can help.

Example: $0.36 + 0.28 + 0.052 + 0.1$

    0.360
    0.280
    0.052
    0.100+
    ‾‾‾‾‾
    0.792
      1

The multiplication of decimals is similar to the multiplication of whole numbers, with an extra step to work out the position of the decimal point (d.p.). The 'golden rule' to find the position is:

Number of d.p.'s in the question = Number of d.p.'s in answer

Example: 4.21×3

    4.21   two decimal places
    3 ×   no decimal places
    ‾‾‾‾
    12.63   two decimal places in the answer.

Example: 0.002×0.03

    0.002   three decimal places
    0.03 ×   two decimal places
    ‾‾‾‾‾
    0.00006   five decimal places in the answer.

Note that all unnecessary zeros should be removed before you multiply the numbers together.

32 Warm-up exercise

Multiply the following decimal numbers. Treat these as whole numbers first and then add the decimal point as a second step:

1 3.2×2.8 *Answer* ....

2 3.08×6.5 *Answer* ....

3 0.095×3.74 *Answer* ....

4 0.002×2.72 (handy hint: place the 0.002 *below* the 2.72)

                                                                          Answer ....

5 10.01×0.15 *Answer* ....

6 500×0.32 (handy hint: multiply 0.32 by 100 and then by 5)

                                                                          Answer ....

7 75×0.04 *Answer* ....

8 33.4×3 *Answer* ....

9 800×2.54 (handy hint: multiply 2.54 by 100 and then by 8)

                                                                          Answer ....

10 4000×3.50 *Answer* ....

The division of decimal numbers is carried out as per whole numbers, while leaving the decimal point in the same position.

Example: $24.369 \div 3$

$$\begin{array}{r} 8.123 \\ 3\overline{)24.369} \end{array}$$ keep the decimal point in the same position when dividing a decimal number

If the number that you are dividing by contains a decimal point, for example 0.35 or 3.5, then it must be *converted to a whole number* before the division can take place. To do this, you must multiply *both* numbers by a power of ten, ie by 10, 100 or 1000 etc, to remove the decimal point from the number that you are dividing by.

Example: $4.5 \div 0.3$ becomes $45 \div 3$ by multiplying *both* numbers by 10 to remove the decimal point from the 0.3

Similarly $9.375 \div 0.02$ becomes $937.5 \div 2$ by multiplying *both* numbers by 100 to remove the decimal point from the 0.02

These divisions can now be carried out as per whole numbers.

33 *Warm-up exercise*

Work out the following division involving decimal numbers. If the number you are *dividing by* contains a decimal point, this must be removed first (questions 4–11):

1   6.8 ÷ 4   *Answer* ....

2   62.25 ÷ 5   *Answer* ....

3   64.25 ÷ 8   *Answer* ....

4   6.8 ÷ 0.04   *Answer* ....

5   9.99 ÷ 0.3   *Answer* ....

6   5.55 ÷ 0.50   *Answer* ....

7   3.6 ÷ 0.6   *Answer* ....

8   9 ÷ 0.15   *Answer* ....

9   1.44 ÷ 1.2   *Answer* ....

10   125 ÷ 0.002   *Answer* ....

11   1000 ÷ 0.05   *Answer* ....

12   0.08 ÷ 5   *Answer* ....

Conversion of decimals to fractions

In order to convert a decimal to a fraction you divide the numbers to the right of the decimal point by:

10 if one number is present
100 if two numbers are present
1000 if three numbers are present etc

then cancel the fraction to its lowest terms. For example:

$$0.5 = \frac{5}{10} = \frac{1}{2}$$

$$0.25 = \frac{25}{100} = \frac{1}{4}$$

$$0.125 = \frac{125}{1000} = \frac{1}{8}$$

34 *Warm-up exercise*

Convert the following decimal numbers to fractions using the method outlined above.

1	0.6	*Answer*		**6**	0.08	*Answer*
2	0.75	*Answer*		**7**	0.95	*Answer*
3	0.625	*Answer*		**8**	1.75	*Answer*
4	0.9	*Answer*		**9**	2.375	*Answer*
5	0.001	*Answer*				

Decimal fractions worth remembering (in ascending size)

0.01 = nought point nought one = one-hundredth = 1/100

0.05 = nought point nought five = one-twentieth = 1/20

0.1 = nought point one = one-tenth = 1/10

0.125 = nought point one two five = one-eighth = 1/8

0.2 = nought point two = one-fifth = 1/5

0.25 = nought point two five = one-quarter = 1/4

0.33 = nought point three three = one-third = 1/3

0.375 = nought point three seven five = three-eighths = 3/8

0.5 = nought point five = one-half = 1/2

0.625 = nought point six two five = five-eighths = 5/8

0.67 = nought point six seven = two-thirds = 2/3

0.75 = nought point seven five = three-quarters = 3/4

0.8 = nought point eight = four-fifths = 4/5

0.9 = nought point nine = nine-tenths = 9/10

Conversion of fractions to decimals

In scientific work it is usually more convenient to express a fraction as a decimal. The method is straightforward. All you have to do is divide the denominator (bottom number) into the numerator (top number).

Example: express $\frac{1}{2}$ as a decimal number

First step: rewrite $\frac{1}{2}$ as $2\overline{)1}$

Second step: rewrite the 1 as 1.0000 by adding a string of zeros

$$2\overline{)1.0000}$$

This division is carried out in the same way as with ordinary numbers, leaving the decimal point in the same position.

2 into 1 won't go so you put a nought down and carry the 1 into the next column to make 10; 2 into 10 goes 5 times.

$$\begin{array}{r} 0.\ 5\ \\ 2\overline{)1.^{1}0000} \end{array}$$

So $\frac{1}{2}$ expressed as a decimal number is 0.5

Example: $\frac{5}{8}$ as a decimal $= 8\overline{)5.0000}$

$$\begin{array}{r} 0.\ 6\ 2\ 5 \\ = 8\overline{)5.^{5}0^{2}0^{4}00} \end{array}$$

$$= 0.625$$

Example: $\frac{7}{400}$ as a decimal $= 400\overline{)7.0000}$

$$\begin{array}{r} 0.\ 01\ \ \ 7\ \ \ 5 \\ = 400\overline{)7.^{7}00^{300}0^{200}0} \end{array}$$

$$= 0.175$$

35 *Warm-up exercise*

Express the following fractions as decimal numbers:

1 $\dfrac{3}{10}$ *Answer* ....

2 $\dfrac{1}{4}$ *Answer* ....

3 $\dfrac{2}{5}$ *Answer* ....

4 $\dfrac{5}{4}$ *Answer* ....

5 $\dfrac{3}{25}$ *Answer* ....

6 $\dfrac{7}{8}$ *Answer* ....

7 $\dfrac{17}{20}$ *Answer* ....

8 $\dfrac{21}{200}$ *Answer* ....

9 $\dfrac{27}{15}$ *Answer* ....

Estimation with decimal numbers

An estimate (or rough idea) of an answer is useful in spotting any wrong answers in multiple choice tests. Take, for example, 3.15×1.92. This can be estimated. To do this, we approximate each of the numbers involved, as follows: 3.15 is approximately 3; 1.92 is approximately 2; so the answer is approximately 6 (3×2). The accurate answer is 6.048. So, we estimate a sum by increasing or decreasing the value of the numbers to give simple numbers that can be worked out in your head.

Example: $87.1 \div 9.2$. Here, we can approximate the 87.1 to 90 and the 9.2 to 9, so $87.1 \div 9.2$ becomes $90 \div 9$ giving an approximate answer of 10.

You can approximate a number to any other number you wish. However, the closer the estimated values are to the actual numbers the more accurate your estimated answer will be. To learn more about approximating, see the earlier section on rounding numbers.

Example: find an estimated answer for the following multiplication: 89×12.2
A very rough estimate for the answer is $100 \times 10 = 1000$
A more accurate estimate for the answer is $90 \times 12 = 1080$
The accurate answer (the actual value) is $89 \times 12.2 = 1085.8$

Estimating an answer in the above way is useful in making sure that your accurate answer is sensible, and therefore, likely to be correct.

36 *Warm-up exercise*

Use approximations to find the correct answers:

1   12.1 × 4.85
   a) 58.69   b) 92.5   c) 70.21   d) 36   *Answer* ....

2   24.1 ÷ 9.6
   a) 4.4   b) 2.51   c) 1.91   d) 3.7   *Answer* ....

3 $\dfrac{94.6 \times 0.51}{24.8}$
   a) 12.7   b) 4   c) 8.64   d) 1.95   *Answer* ....

37 *Warm-up exercise*

Work out the following problems:

1   1.5897 × 1000   *Answer* ....

2   31.729 × 100   *Answer* ....

3   17.1703 × 1000   *Answer* ....

4   7692105 ÷ 10000   *Answer* ....

5   0.175 ÷ 1000   *Answer* ....

6   0.0058 ÷ 1000   *Answer* ....

7   Multiply 5.5 by 6   *Answer* ....

8   Multiply 22.75 by 4   *Answer* ....

9   Divide 120 by 0.05   *Answer* ....

Calculating percentages

A percentage (percentage sign is %) means 'out of one hundred'; in other words, something is split into a hundred equal parts and each part is one per cent. A percentage is basically a special case of a fraction. *All* percentage fractions have the same denominator, which is 100. All that changes is the top number. For example:

$$3\% = \frac{3}{100} \ (3 \div 100) \qquad\qquad 99\% = \frac{99}{100} \ (99 \div 100)$$

A percentage fraction can be cancelled to its lowest terms:

$$40\% = \frac{40}{100} \ (40 \div 100) \text{ which cancels to } \frac{4}{10} \text{ and finally to } \frac{2}{5}$$

$$12\% = \frac{12}{100} \ (12 \div 100) \text{ which cancels to } \frac{6}{50} \text{ and finally to } \frac{3}{25}$$

Percentages can also be written in decimal form. To do this we divide the percentage by 100, expressing the answer as a decimal. The easiest way to divide by 100 is to move the decimal point two places to the left. For example:

40% as a decimal: $40.0 \div 100 = 0.4$

Similarly, 99% as a decimal: $99.0 \div 100 = 0.99$

Similarly, 3% as a decimal: $03.0 \div 100 = 0.03$

How do you work out the percentage of something? To do this you must multiply the 'something' by the percentage fraction. For example:

Find 25% of 60

First step: $25\% = \frac{25}{100} = \frac{1}{4}$ $\qquad$ Second step: $\frac{1}{4} \times 60 = \frac{60}{4} = 15$

Another method is to convert the percentage to a decimal fraction as a first step. For example:

Find 25% of 60
First step: $25\% = 25 \div 100 = 0.25$ $\qquad$ Second step: $0.25 \times 60 = 15$

In the above example, the fraction method of working out the answer was easier than the decimal method but in some cases the reverse is true.

How to express numbers as percentages

We have seen that percentage means out of 100, so:

$$100\% = \frac{100}{100} = 1$$

This means that we can write any number as a percentage, without affecting its value, by multiplying it by 100%, ie by 1.

Whole numbers can be converted to percentages as follows:

$$2 \times 100\% = 200\% \text{ (ie 2 wholes is 200\%)}$$
$$\text{Similarly } 10 \times 100\% = 1000\% \text{ (ie 10 wholes is 1000\%)}$$

Fractions can be converted to percentages in the same way. For example:

Example: $\frac{1}{4} \times 100\% = 25\%$ similarly $\frac{3}{10} \times 100\% = 30\%$

Decimal fractions can be converted to percentages in the same way, ie by multiplying by 100%, for example:

$0.15 \times 100\% = 15\%$ $0.01 \times 100\% = 1\%$
$0.995 \times 100\% = 99.5\%$ $1.1 \times 100\% = 110\%$

Working out percentage change from the original number

Sometimes you will have to compare old and new figures in terms of a percentage change. The change is always calculated as a percentage of the original number, not the final number. For example:

A new car is priced at £20,000. After one year the value has dropped to £14,000. Find the percentage depreciation in terms of the original cost.

After one year the car is worth £14,000.

So it depreciates by $20000 - 14000 = 6000$

$$\% \text{ depreciation} = \frac{\text{depreciation}}{\text{original cost}} \times 100\%$$

$$= \frac{6000}{20000} \times 100\%$$

$$= \frac{6}{20} \times 100\% = \frac{3}{10} \times 100\% = 30\%$$

Find the percentage increase in price if the price rises from £60 to £75.

Increase in price = 75 − 60 = £15

$$\% \text{ increase} = \frac{\text{increase in price}}{\text{original price}} \times 100\%$$

$$= \frac{15}{60} \times 100\% = 25\%$$

Find the percentage decrease in price when the price drops from £75 to £60.

$$\% \text{ decrease} = \frac{\text{decrease in price}}{\text{original price}} \times 100\%$$

$$= \frac{15}{75} \times 100\% = 20\%$$

Note how £60 to £75 is a 25% increase whereas £75 to £60 is a 20% decrease, even though the change is £15 in both instances; this is because of the different starting values (denominators).

Working out the original price from the percentage change

It is easy to work out the new price when you know the percentage change but working out the original price from the new price requires a little more thought.

In the first instance (working out the new price) you simply multiply the new price by the percentage discount subtracted from 100%. For example:

An e-book reader is priced at £169. The price is reduced by 20% in a sale. What is the sale price?

£169 × (100 − 20)% = £169 × 80% = £169 × 0.8 = £135.20

Alternatively, you can work out how much the 20% price reduction comes to before subtracting it from the full price: £169 × 20% = £169 × 0.2 = £33.80 discount, then the sale price is given by £169 − £33.80 = £135.20 as before.

38 Warm-up exercise

Convert the following percentages to both fractions AND decimals:

1	20%	*Answer*		**6**	45%	*Answer*
2	25%	*Answer*		**7**	35%	*Answer*
3	10%	*Answer*		**8**	22%	*Answer*
4	75%	*Answer*		**9**	2%	*Answer*
5	90%	*Answer*				

Work out the following percentages using either the fractions method or the decimal method.

Use the fractions method:

10   50% of 180   *Answer* ....

11   30% of 200   *Answer* ....

12   10% of 250   *Answer* ....

13   5% of 250   *Answer* ....

Use the decimal method:

14   62.5% of 200   *Answer* ....

15 $2\frac{1}{2}$% of 1000   *Answer* ....

Convert each decimal or fraction to a percentage by multiplying it by 100%:

16   0.5   *Answer* ....   **21**   0.005   *Answer* ....

17   0.015   *Answer* ....   **22** $\frac{1}{5}$ *Answer* ....

18   0.75   *Answer* ....   **23** $\frac{9}{25}$ *Answer* ....

19   1.05   *Answer* ....   **24** $\frac{1}{8}$ *Answer* ....

20   1.0   *Answer* ....   **25** $\frac{17}{20}$ *Answer* ....

Find the percentage change in going from:

26   £100 to £150   *Answer* ....

27   £50 to £30   *Answer* ....

28   £150 to £60   *Answer* ....

29   £75.00 to £56.25   *Answer* ....

30   If 20% of applicants fail a test, how many applicants
         pass the test if there are 32400 test takers?   *Answer* ....

Time

Candidates should be familiar with both the 12-hour clock and the 24-hour clock, which starts and finishes at midnight, ie midnight = 0000 hours or 2400 hours (twenty-four hundred hours); noon (midday) = 1200 hrs (twelve hundred hours).

Times can be converted from the 12-hour clock to the 24-hour clock by re-writing the time as a four-digit number and adding 12 hours to all pm times. For example:

9.30 am = 0930 hrs (O nine-thirty hours)
3 pm = 3 + 12 hrs = 1500 hrs (fifteen hundred hours)
10.55 pm = 10.55 + 12 hrs = 2255 (twenty-two fifty-five hours)

Always use this four-digit format when responding to QTS questions; there is no need to include the word 'hours' in your answers.

Fractional parts of an hour are converted to minutes by multiplying the fraction (or its decimal) by 60 minutes:

$\frac{1}{4}$ hr = 0.25 hr = 0.25 × 60 = 15 min
$\frac{1}{10}$ hr = 0.1 hr = 0.1 × 60 = 6 min

You can add or subtract times as follows:

1445 hrs + 1 hr 50 min = 1445 + 2 hr − 10 min = 1635 hrs
2235 hrs − 55 min = 2235 hrs − 1 hr + 5 min = 2140 hrs
3.5 hr + 10 min = 3 hr + 30 min + 10 min = 3 hr 40 min
4 hr ÷ 6 = 4 × 60 ÷ 6 = 4 × 10 = 40 min

Money

Always use the decimal point format when answering QTS questions that involve money; the currency sign is optional. For example:

£3.45 + 65 pence = 345p + 65p = 410p = £4.10, or
£3.45 + 65 pence = £3.45 + £0.65 = £4.10

There is no need to include a letter 'p' after the pence if you include a pound sign (£).

Calculations that involve different currencies require that you either multiply or divide by the exchange rate. For example:

If £1 = 2.25 Swiss francs (CHF), how many Swiss francs are there in £60?
£1 = 2.25 Swiss francs (CHF) then £60 = 60 × 2.25 CHF
   = 60 × 2 + 60 × $\frac{1}{4}$
   = 120 + 15 = 135 CHF

If £1 = 2.25 Swiss francs (CHF), how many pounds are there in 90 CHF?

> 90 CHF = 90 ÷ 2.25 pounds
> multiply 2.25 × 4 (removes the decimal point) to give 9
> then multiply 90 × 4 to match, ie:
> 90 ÷ 2.25 = 90 × 4 ÷ 9 = 10 × 4 = £40
> (check: 40 × 2.25 = 80 + 10 = 90)

Speed, distance and time

For the purposes of travel, speed is measured in miles per hour (mph) or kilometres per hour (km/h), distance is measured in miles or kilometres, and time is measured in hours, minutes and seconds, though you will also be familiar with days, weeks, months and years. At the start of this section, distance, speed and time calculations are considered without reference to any equations; non-formula methods are useful when calculators are not allowed. The latter part of the section looks at the distance–speed–time triangle as an aid to choosing the correct formula when working out more difficult problems.

Distance

Distance is speed times time. However, we can replace a difficult multiplication with simple arithmetic steps. We do this by considering what happens in *1 hour* (the unitary method) and then what happens for longer or shorter periods in relation to 1 hour.

Example: a coach travels a constant speed of 40 miles per hour for 2 hours and 45 minutes. What distance will it cover?

> Consider 1 hour: *40 miles in 1 hour*
> 80 miles in 2 hours (40 × 2)
> 20 miles in 30 minutes (40 × ½)
> 10 miles in 15 minutes (40 × ¼)
> So total = 110 miles in 2 hours and 45 minutes

Example: a cyclist travels at a constant speed of 12 mph for 20 minutes. How far will the cyclist travel?

> Consider 1 hour: *12 miles in 1 hour*
> So 4 miles travelled in 20 minutes (12 ÷ 3)

The time period of 20 minutes is one-third of an hour so we multiply 12 miles by one-third; alternatively, we can see that there are three periods of 20 minutes in 1 hour, so we simply divide 12 miles by three to give 4 miles (which is the same as multiplying by one-third).

To make distance calculations quickly, it helps if you can convert times in minutes to fractions of one hour (60 minutes) easily. A list of common fractions is shown below. To calculate the distance travelled in a given time, you multiply the distance travelled in 1 hour by the appropriate fraction of 1 hour (or you divide by the number of time periods in 1 hour).

For 30 minutes (2 periods per hour):	multiply distance by $\frac{1}{2}$ (or divide by 2)
20 minutes (3 periods per hour):	multiply distance by $\frac{1}{3}$ (or divide by 3)
15 minutes (4 periods per hour):	multiply distance by $\frac{1}{4}$ (or divide by 4)
12 minutes (5 periods per hour):	multiply distance by $\frac{1}{5}$ (or divide by 5)
10 minutes (6 periods per hour):	multiply distance by $\frac{1}{6}$ (or divide by 6)
6 minutes (10 periods per hour):	multiply distance by $\frac{1}{10}$ (or divide by 10)
5 minutes (12 periods per hour):	multiply distance by $\frac{1}{12}$ (or divide by 12)
4 minutes (15 periods per hour):	multiply distance by $\frac{1}{15}$ (or divide by 15)
3 minutes (20 periods per hour):	multiply distance by $\frac{1}{20}$ (or divide by 20)
2 minutes (30 periods per hour):	multiply distance by $\frac{1}{30}$ (or divide by 30)
1 minute (60 periods per hour):	multiply distance by $\frac{1}{60}$ (or divide by 60)

For less obvious times we can use combinations of known times, for example: 26 minutes = 20 minutes (divide by 3) + 6 minutes (divide by 10).

Example: how far will you travel in 26 minutes at 45 mph? Split 26 minutes into 20 minutes and 6 minutes, then we have:

> 45 *miles in 1 hour*
> 15 miles in 20 minutes
> + 4.5 miles in 6 minutes
> = 19.5 miles in 26 minutes

Example: how far will a cyclist travel in 42 minutes if he cycles at a constant speed of 10 mph? Split 42 minutes into 30 minutes and 12 minutes, then we have:

> 10 *miles in 1 hour*
> 5 miles in 30 minutes
> + 2 miles in 12 minutes
> = 7 miles in 42 minutes

39 *Warm-up exercise*

1   How far will a car travel in 10 minutes at a constant speed of 66 mph?

Answer ....

2   How far will a cyclist travel in 5 minutes at a constant speed of 12 mph?

Answer ....

3   How far will a coach travel at 40 mph in 15 minutes?

Answer ....

4   How far will a pedestrian travel at 3 mph for 40 minutes?

Answer ....

5   How far will you travel at 10 mph for 2 hours and 15 minutes?

Answer ....

6   How far will you travel at 24 km per hour for 25 minutes?

Answer ....

7   How far does a plane travel in 1 minute at a speed of 780 mph?

Answer ....

8   How far does a ferry travel in 2.25 hours at 36 mph?

Answer ....

Converting between kilometres and miles

You will always be told how to convert from 'distances in miles to distances in kilometres', and vice versa. However, the basics are worth remembering. A mile is approximately 1600 metres, and a kilometre is 1000 metres, so 1 mile = 1.6 kilometres; multiplying both sides of the equation by five gives 5 miles = 8 kilometres, so 1 kilometre = 5/8 mile (approximately 0.62 miles).

Many calculations that require a conversion will make use of the 5/8 ratio, as in:

5 miles = 8 km; 10 miles = 16 km; 20 miles = 32 km; 25 miles = 40 km; 50 miles = 80 km; 100 miles = 160 km etc

Example: a school bus makes a round trip of 32 km. How far is this in miles if one kilometre is equivalent to five-eighths of a mile?

1 km = 5/8 mile
8 km = 5 miles
16 km = 10 miles
32 km = 20 miles

Example: a student walks 2 miles to university. How far is this in kilometres if 5 miles are equivalent to 8 kilometres?

5 miles = 8 km
1 mile = 8/5 km = 1.6 km
2 miles = 3.2 km

Example: a pupil travels 15.6 km to school. What is this distance in miles if 1 mile is equivalent to 1.6 km?

1 mile = 1.6 km
5 miles = 8 km
1 km = 5/8 mile

$$15.6 \text{ km} = 15.6 \times 5/8 = 78/8 = 9\frac{6}{8} = 9\frac{3}{4} \text{ miles}$$

40 *Warm-up exercise*

1   If 1 km is approximately 0.62 miles, how far is 30 kilometres in miles?

   Answer ....

2   A school coach makes a journey of 320 km.
   How far is this in miles if one kilometre is five-eighths of a mile?

   Answer ....

3   A school coach makes a journey of 360 km.
   How far is this in miles if one kilometre is five-eighths of a mile?

   Answer ....

4   A cyclist covers a distance of 1.5 miles.
   How far is this in kilometres if 5 miles are equivalent to 8 km?

   Answer ....

Speed

To calculate the speed you need to know the distance travelled and the time taken. Speeds use miles per hour or kilometres per hour, so if we find the distance travelled in 1 hour (the *unitary* method) then this is the speed.

Example: what is our speed if we cover 96 miles in 1 hour and 20 minutes?

   We need to find the distance travelled in 1 hour.

   We have: 96 miles in 1 hour 20 minutes
                 96 miles in 80 minutes
                 48 miles in 40 minutes
                 24 miles in 20 minutes
   Total: 72 miles in 60 minutes

   Or 72 miles in 1 hour = 72 *mph*

Example: a journey of 5 kilometres takes 24 minutes at a constant speed. Calculate the speed in kilometres per hour (km/h).

   Again we need to find the distance travelled in 1 hour (60 minutes).

   We have: 5 km in 24 minutes
                 2.5 km in 12 minutes

Choosing the period of 12 minutes is helpful because there are five periods of 12 minutes in 1 hour (see earlier), so we can multiply 2.5 by 5 to find the *distance we would have covered had the journey lasted 1 hour.*

$$5\,km\ in\ 12\,min\ = 2.5 \times 5\,km\ in\ 1\ hour$$
$$= (2 \times 5) + (0.5 \times 5)$$
$$= 10 + 2.5\,km\ in\ 1\ hour$$
$$= 12.5\,km\ in\ 1\ hour = \mathit{12.5\,km/h}$$

Example: what speed covers 250 km in 2 hours and 30 minutes?

We need to find the distance travelled in 1 hour (60 minutes).

We have: 250 km in 2 hours 30 minutes
           500 km in 5 hours
           100 km in 1 hour = *100 km/h*

Here we doubled the time to remove the half hour.

Example: what speed covers 240 km in 2 hours and 40 minutes?

We need to find the distance travelled in 1 hour (60 minutes).

We have: 240 km in 2 hours 40 minutes
           240 km in 160 minutes
           120 km in 80 minutes
           60 km in 40 minutes
           30 km in 20 minutes
Total: *90 km/h*

Example: what speed covers 240 km in 2 hours and 40 minutes?

Alternative method:

We need to find the distance travelled in 1 hour (60 minutes).
We have: 240 km in 2 hours 40 minutes
Multiply by three: 720 km in 6 hours 120 minutes
                    720 km in 8 hours = *90 km/h*

Here we tripled the time so that the minutes would be divisible by 60, giving us a whole number of hours.

41 *Warm-up exercise*

1   What speed covers 84 miles in 3 hours?

Answer ....

2   What speed covers 25 miles in 30 minutes?

Answer ....

3   What speed covers 7 miles in 10 minutes?

Answer ....

4   What speed covers 21 km in 45 minutes?

Answer ....

5   What speed covers 140 km in 2 hours and 20 minutes?

Answer ....

6   What speed covers 12 miles in 40 minutes?

Answer ....

7   What speed covers 16 miles in 15 minutes?

Answer ....

8   What speed covers 27 km in 45 minutes?

Answer ....

9   What speed covers 132 km in 1 hour and 50 minutes?

Answer ....

Time

You should be able to express any period of time in a smaller or larger unit based on the conversions shown below:

60 seconds (s) = 1 minute (min); seconds to minutes = divide by 60

60 minutes (min) = 1 hour (h, hr); minutes to hours = divide by 60

24 hours = 1 day (d); hours to days = divide by 24; 28, 29, 30 or 31 days = 1 month; 365 days = 1 year; 366 days = 1 leap year

13 weeks = 1 quarter; 52 weeks = 1 year; 12 months = 1 year

p.a. = per annum = per year; am = before noon; pm = afternoon

GMT = Greenwich Mean Time

Candidates should be familiar with both the 12-hour clock (which has two 12-hour periods – am and pm) and the 24-hour clock, which finishes at 2400 hours (twenty-four hundred hours), which is the same time as 0000 (zero hundred hours) the following day; noon (midday) = 1200 hrs (twelve hundred hours).

Times can be converted from the 12-hour clock to the 24-hour clock by rewriting the time as a four-digit number and adding 12 hours to all pm times. For example:

8.30 am = 0830 hrs (O eight thirty hours)
1 pm = 1 + 12 hrs = 1300 hrs (thirteen hundred hours)
10.45 pm = 10.45 + 12 hrs = 2245 (twenty-two forty-five hours)

Likewise, times on the 24-hour clock can be converted to 12-hour clock times by subtracting 12 hours from all afternoon times (ie those greater than 1200 hrs); for example, 2050 hours = 2050 – 12 hrs = 8.50 pm.

Example: a school coach arrived at the Tate Gallery at 1300 hours. The journey took 1 hour and 55 minutes, excluding a 25-minute break. What time was it when the coach set out?

Total time taken = 1 hour 55 minutes + 25 minutes break = 2 hrs 20 min; (here you add 5 minutes to get to 2 hours and then add the remaining 20 minutes to get to 2 hours and 20 minutes). So we know that the coach must have set out 2 hours and 20 minutes before its arrival time of 1300 hrs. Subtracting hours and minutes in a single step is not easy, so *subtract more time than you need, in complete hours, and then add back the extra minutes* as follows: 1300 hrs – 2 hrs 20 min is 1300 hrs – 3 hrs + 40 min = 1000 hrs 40 min or 1040 hours.

42 *Warm-up exercise*

1   How many seconds are there in eight and three-quarter minutes?

Answer ....

2   How many minutes are there in three hours and twenty-five minutes?

Answer ....

3   How many days are there in 168 hours?   *Answer* ....

4   Convert 6.30 am to a 24-hour clock time.   *Answer* ....

5   Convert 9.15 pm to a 24-hour clock time.   *Answer* ....

6   Convert 2245 hours to a 12-hour clock time.   *Answer* ....

7   Add 3 hours and 25 minutes to 1445 hours.   *Answer* ....

8   Subtract 1 hour and 42 minutes from 1410 hrs.   *Answer* ....

43 *Easy questions*

1   A school coach arrives at the Tate Gallery at twelve hundred hours. The journey took two hours and twenty-five minutes excluding a fifteen-minute break. At what time did the coach set out?

Answer ....

2   An exam finished at twelve twenty-five hours having lasted one and three-quarter hours. At what time did the exam start?

Answer ....

3   Teachers at a school have four hours and twelve minutes of contact time per day. What is the contact time per week?

Answer ....

4   A pupil aged eleven years and four months has a reading age eighteen months below his actual age. What is his reading age?

Answer ....

5   A school day starts at eight-fifty am and finishes at three-thirty pm Breaks total one hour and fifteen minutes. What is the maximum number of half-hour lessons possible per day?

Answer ....

6   School lessons start at a quarter past nine. There are ten lessons per day lasting thirty minutes each and breaks that total ninety minutes. What time does the school day finish?

Answer ....

7   A school day ends at five past three. There are two lessons in the afternoon each lasting fifty minutes with a ten-minute break in between. At what time does the first afternoon lesson begin?

Answer ....

To calculate the time for a journey you need to know the distance travelled and the speed of travel. The methods employed to calculate time using 'a non-formula' method are similar to those to calculate speed, in that we start with a time period of 1 hour (unitary method), but instead of calculating the distance travelled in 1 hour (the speed) we calculate the time taken to cover the required distance.

Example: how long will it take to travel 144 miles at 36 mph?

> We have: 36 miles in 1 hour
> 72 miles in 2 hours
> 144 miles in 4 hours

Example: how long will it take to travel 14 km at 42 km/h?

> We have: 42 km in 1 hour
> 21 km 30 minutes
> 7 km in 10 minutes
> = 14 km in 20 minutes

The alternative method of solving distance, speed and time calculations is to use the following three equations or formulae:

$$\text{Speed} = \frac{\text{Distance}}{\text{Time}} \qquad \text{Time} = \frac{\text{Distance}}{\text{Speed}} \qquad \text{Distance} = \text{Speed} \times \text{Time}$$

$$S = \frac{D}{T} \qquad\qquad T = \frac{D}{S} \qquad\qquad D = S \times T$$

If your algebra is up to scratch, you need only remember that 'distance is speed times time', because you can manipulate this equation to get either Time on its own (divide both sides by Speed) or Speed on its own (divide both sides by Time). However, many candidates will find it easier to refer to the distance–speed–time triangle.

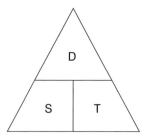

Example (used earlier): how long will it take to travel 14 km at 42 km/h?

To use the triangle, place the tip of your finger over the *variable* you need, in this case Time, to leave 'Distance over Speed', meaning Distance divided by Speed.

$$T = \frac{D}{S} = \frac{14}{42} = \frac{7}{21} = \frac{1}{3}\ \text{hour} = 20\ \text{minutes}$$

44 *Easy questions*

Use the SDT triangle where necessary. Take 1 mile to be 1.6 km:

1   What distance is covered in 4 hours and 20 minutes at 60 mph?

Answer ....

2   What distance is covered in 4 hours and 20 minutes at 72 mph?

Answer ....

3   A school trip to the Tate Gallery took two hours and fifteen minutes by coach, travelling at an average speed of forty miles per hour. How far away was the Gallery?

Answer ....

4   What speed in miles per hour covers 44 kilometres in 30 minutes?

Answer ....

5   What speed in kilometres per hour covers 17.5 miles in 35 minutes?

Answer ....

6   What speed in miles per hour covers 66 kilometres in 45 minutes?

Answer ....

7   What time will it take to travel 6 miles at a speed of 6 kilometres per hour?

Answer ....

8   How long will it take to drive 140 km at 70 mph?

Answer ....

9   A coach leaves Birmingham at 1130 hrs. What time will it arrive at Manchester airport, 80 miles away, if it averages 60 mph?

Answer ....

Average speed for two journeys at different speeds

Care needs to be taken when calculating average speeds. If a car travels from A to B at 40 mph and then from B to A at 60 mph, the average speed might appear to be 50 mph; however, this is not the case. Average speed is calculated as follows:

$$\text{Average speed} = \frac{\text{Total distance travelled}}{\text{Total time taken}}$$

Example: a car travels from A to B, a distance of 80 miles, at a constant speed of 40 mph, and then returns from B to A at a constant speed of 60 mph. What was the average speed?

Method:

Divide total distance by total time:

i)   total distance = 80 + 80 = 160 miles

ii)   total time = time to travel from A to B and time to travel from B to A

For A to B: $T = \dfrac{D}{S} = \dfrac{80}{40} = 2$ hours

For B to A: $T = \dfrac{D}{S} = \dfrac{80}{60} = \dfrac{8}{6} = \dfrac{4}{3} = 1\dfrac{1}{3}$ hour

Total time = A to B added to B to A = $2 + 1\dfrac{1}{3} = 3\dfrac{1}{3}$ hrs

Total distance = 160 miles

Average speed = total distance ÷ total time

$$= 160 \div 3\frac{1}{3} = 160 \div \frac{10}{3} = 160 \times \frac{3}{10} = 16 \times 3 = 48 \ mph$$

45 *More difficult question*

1   A coach travels from Chester to Liverpool at 36 mph before returning to Chester at 28 mph. If the distance between the two cities is 33.6 kilometres, calculate, by any method:

a)   the distance from Chester to Liverpool in miles, if 5 miles are equivalent to 8 kilometres;

Answer ....

b)   the average speed for the round trip.

Answer ....

Introduction to the mental arithmetic questions

The first section of the test is an aural mental arithmetic test heard through the computer's headphones. Each question is read out twice with no pause in between. You will then be given 18 seconds in which to enter your answer using the keyboard before the next question is read out. You are not allowed to use a calculator but you will have access to a pen and paper to jot down the calculation. The following points are worth noting:

● Write down any numbers and attempt the question straight away without waiting for it to be read out a second time. There is less time to spare than you might think.

● Do not continue with any question beyond the allotted time. Leave it and move on to the next question. Do not pursue any answer at the expense of missing the next question.

● Most questions will involve more than one arithmetic process (eg multiplication followed by division or cancelling).

● There are no right and wrong methods. Your answers will be marked by a computer. This book contains tips and exemplar methods but you should use any arithmetic techniques that work for you.

● The context of the question is irrelevant to the maths involved. You simply apply the four arithmetic operations of addition, subtraction, multiplication and division to fractions, decimals, percentages, time, money and measurements.

There now follows a mental arithmetic exemplar test and five similar tests with answers at the end of the book. You will need a pen and paper but not a calculator. You can simulate the actual test more accurately by having someone read the questions out aloud for you or by recording the questions and then playing them back.

Exemplar test with answers

1   In a school of one hundred and eighty-five pupils, one-fifth take free school meals. How many take free school meals?

$185 \div 5 = 200 \div 5 - 15 \div 5 = 40 - 3 = \mathbf{37}$

2   A school library contains two hundred and fifty-two books. If the ratio of non-fiction to fiction books is five to one, how many fiction books are there?

$5n + n = 252; 6n = 252; n = 240 \div 6 + 12 \div 6 = 40 + 2 = \mathbf{42}$

3   If one gallon is equivalent to four point five litres, how many gallons are there in three litres? Give your answer as a fraction.

1 gal = 4.5 l; so 1 l = $1 \div 4.5$; 3 l = $3 \div 4.5 = 30 \div 45 = \mathbf{2/3}$

4   A school can buy twenty books at seven pounds and fifty pence each or borrow the books from a library service at a cost of fifty pounds. How much money will be saved by borrowing the books?

$20 \times £7.50 = 2 \times £75 = £150; £150 - 50 = \mathbf{£100}$

5   A school audio CD costs five pounds seventy-five plus VAT. If VAT is charged at twenty per cent how much does the CD cost to the nearest penny?

$20\% = 1/5$; 575 pence $\div 5 = 115$ pence $= £1.15 + £5.75 = \mathbf{£6.90}$

6   Three hundred and twenty pupils sat GCSE English. If sixty-five per cent of the pupils achieved grade C or below, how many achieved grade B or above?

$100\% - 65\% = 35\%; 35\% \times 320 = 0.35 \times 320 = 3.5 \times 32$
$= 3 \times 32 + 0.5 \times 32 = 96 + 16 = \mathbf{112}$

7   What is sixty-two and one-half per cent as a fraction?

$62.5\% = 62.5/100 = 125/200 = 25/40 = \mathbf{5/8}$

8   A school coach arrived at the Tate Gallery at thirteen hundred hours. The journey took one hour and thirty-five minutes excluding a fifteen-minute break. What time was it when the coach set out?

Total time taken = 1 hrs 35 min + 15 min = 1 hr 50 min
1300 hrs − 1 hr 50 min = 1300 hrs − 2 hr + 10 min = **1110** hrs

9   In a school run a pupil completed three miles around a four hundred metre track. How many laps of the track were completed if one mile is equivalent to one point six kilometres?

3 miles = 3 × 1.6 = 4.8 km
4.8 km × 1000 m/km = 48 × 100 m = 4800 m
4800 ÷ 400 = 48 ÷ 4 = **12**

10   A ski trip to Switzerland costs six hundred pounds and requires a deposit of thirty per cent. What is the deposit in Swiss francs if one pound is equivalent to two Swiss francs?

£600 × 30% = £600 × 0.3 = £60 × 3 = £180
£180 × 2 Swiss francs per pound = **360** francs

11   A school playground measures sixteen metres by twelve point five metres. What is its area in metres squared?

16 × 12.5 = 16 × 10 + 16 × 2.5 = 160 + 40 = **200**
(16 × 2.5 = 16 × 2 + 16 × 0.5 = 32 + 8 = 40)

12   An 11–18 comprehensive school has fifteen hundred pupils on roll, including one hundred and eighty A-level students. What percentage of the pupils on roll are A-level students?

180 ÷ 1500 × 100% = 180 ÷ 15 × 1% = (150 ÷ 15) + (30 ÷ 15) = **12%**

Mental arithmetic tests 1–5

Mental arithmetic test 1 (time allowed = 10 minutes)

1   In a school of three hundred and twenty-four pupils, one-sixth take free school meals. How many take free school meals?

2   A school library contains one hundred and fifty-six books. If the number of non-fiction books is twice the number of fiction books, how many non-fiction books are there?

3   If one gallon is equivalent to four point five litres, how many gallons are there in one litre? Give your answer as a fraction.

4   A school can buy ten books at nine pounds and ninety-five pence each or borrow the books from a library service at a cost of forty pounds. How much money will be saved by borrowing the books?

5   A school audio CD costs six pounds sixty pence plus VAT. If VAT is charged at twenty per cent, how much does the CD cost to the nearest penny?

6   Two hundred and forty pupils sat GCSE English. If forty-five per cent of the pupils achieved grade D or below, how many achieved grade C or above?

7   A school bus arrives at the Tate Gallery at twelve hundred hours. The journey took two hours and twenty-five minutes excluding a fifteen-minute break. At what time did it set out?

8   In a school run a pupil completed five miles around a four hundred metre track. How many laps of the track were completed if one mile is equivalent to one point six kilometres?

9   A ski trip to Switzerland costs seven hundred and fifty pounds and requires a twenty per cent deposit. What is the deposit in Swiss francs if one pound is equivalent to two Swiss francs?

10   What is thirty-seven and one-half per cent as a fraction?

11   A school playground measures twelve metres by thirteen point five metres. What is its area in metres squared?

12   An 11–18 comprehensive school has fifteen hundred and fifty pupils on roll, including three hundred and ten A-level students. What percentage of the pupils on roll are A-level students?

Mental arithmetic test 2 (time allowed = 10 minutes)

1   School dinners cost one pound and eighty-five pence each. A pupil pays in advance for a week's dinners. What is the correct change in pence out of a ten pound note?

2   A school with nine hundred and fifty places has an occupancy rate of ninety-four per cent. How many more pupils could it take?

3   A school has two hundred and ninety boys and three hundred and ten girls. How many girls would you expect there to be in a representative sample of one hundred and twenty pupils?

4   An exam finished at twelve twenty-five hours having lasted one and three-quarter hours. At what time did the exam start?

5   In a sponsored run a pupil completed eighteen laps around a four hundred metre track. How many miles did he complete if one kilometre equals five-eighths of a mile?

6   In a secondary school with nine hundred pupils, four out of every five pupils own a mobile phone. How many pupils do not own a mobile phone?

7   A sponsored walk by five hundred pupils raised six thousand, nine hundred and fifty pounds for charity. What was the average amount raised per pupil?

8   A school trip to the Tate Gallery took two hours and fifteen minutes by coach, travelling at an average speed of forty miles per hour. How far away was the gallery?

9   A pupil gained thirty marks out of fifty in one Maths test and sixteen marks out of twenty-five in a second Maths test. What was the average percentage for the two tests assuming they were weighted equally?

10   What is sixty-two and one-half per cent as a decimal fraction to one decimal place?

11   A school skiing trip costs seven hundred and twenty pounds per pupil with a fifteen per cent deposit. How much is the deposit in Euros if there are one point two-five Euros to the pound?

12   Teachers at a school have four hours and twelve minutes contact time per day. What is the contact time per week?

Mental arithmetic test 3 (time allowed = 10 minutes)

1   A pupil aged eleven years and four months has a reading age eighteen months below his actual age. What is his reading age?

2   A geography school trip costs seventy pounds and the deposit is fourteen pounds. What percentage of the cost is the deposit?

3   Out of one hundred and forty-four pupils who sat GCSE English Literature, ninety achieved grades A to C. What fraction achieved grades A to C?

4   In a primary school, five per cent of half-day sessions were missed through absence. If there were three hundred and eighty half-day sessions, how many were missed through absence?

5   How many school books at eight pounds and seventy-five pence each can be bought on a budget of one hundred pounds?

6   The highest mark in a Maths test was forty-six correct answers out of fifty questions and the lowest mark was twenty-five correct answers out of fifty questions. What is the difference between the highest and lowest marks in percentage points?

7   A ski trip to Switzerland costs eight hundred pounds per pupil and requires a twenty-five per cent deposit. What is the deposit in Swiss francs if one hundred pounds buys two hundred and five Swiss francs?

8   What is four-fifths as a percentage?

9   A fence is to be erected around a school playing field. The field is rectangular in shape and measures one hundred and twenty metres by ninety metres. What length of fence will be needed?

10   What is two point five per cent as a fraction in its lowest terms?

11   The teacher to pupil ratio on a school trip is not to be less than one to fifteen. If there are one hundred and seventy-two pupils going on the trip, how many teachers will be required?

12   A school day starts at eight-fifty am and finishes at three-thirty pm. Breaks total one hour and fifteen minutes. What is the maximum number of half-hour lessons possible per day?

Mental arithmetic test 4 (time allowed = 10 minutes)

1   At the start of a school day the library contains twelve thousand books. By the end of the day one hundred and twenty-three books have been loaned out and fifty-seven books have been returned. How many books are there in the library at the end of the day?

2   In a class of twenty-five pupils, forty per cent are girls. How many boys are there in the class?

3   GCSE pupils take a Double Science or Single Science award. If Double Science is seven times more popular than the Single Science, what fraction of the pupils take Single Science?

4   The cost of a school ski trip was six hundred and sixty pounds per pupil last year. This year the cost will increase by three per cent. What will be the cost per pupil this year? Give your answer to the nearest pound.

5   What is zero point four five as a fraction?

6   In a year group, seven out of every ten pupils achieved Key Stage 2. What percentage of the pupils failed to achieve Key Stage 2?

7   How many pieces of card measuring thirty centimetres by twenty centimetres can be cut from a sheet measuring one point five metres by one point one metres?

8   A pupil is one point six metres tall. If there are two point five centimetres to the inch, how tall is the pupil in inches?

9   School lessons start at a quarter past nine. There are ten lessons per day lasting thirty minutes each and breaks that total ninety minutes. What time does the school day finish?

10   A school minibus averages thirty miles per gallon. A teacher fills the tank with forty-five litres of fuel. How far can the minibus travel if one gallon is equivalent to four and one-half litres?

11   A test has a pass mark of seventy per cent. If there are thirty-five questions, what is the minimum number of correct answers necessary to pass the test?

12   In a school of one hundred and ninety-two pupils, seven-twelfths are boys. How many girls are there?

Mental arithmetic test 5 (time allowed = 10 minutes)

1   Four hundred and twenty-four pupils in a year group sit GCSE Maths. If seventy-nine pupils failed to achieve grade C or above, how many pupils did achieve grade C or above?

2   The cost of a school trip to France was four hundred and thirty pounds last year. This year the trip will cost eleven per cent more. What will be the cost of the trip this year?

3   GCSE pupils take Triple, Double or Single Science. If three-quarters take the Double Science and one-sixth take Single Science, how many take Triple Science?

4   A school charges six pence per A4 page for photocopying, thirty pence for binding and twenty-five pence for a clear cover. What is the cost of two one-hundred-page books bound with clear front and back covers?

5   What is twenty-two point five per cent as a decimal fraction?

6   The average weight of a class of eleven-year-old pupils is forty kilograms. What is this in pounds if one kilogram is equivalent to two point two pounds?

7   A school teacher hires a minibus at fifty pounds per day plus the cost of the petrol used. The minibus uses one litre of fuel for every ten kilometres travelled. If fuel costs one pound and fifty pence per litre, how much would it cost for a one-day round trip of two hundred kilometres?

8   The pass mark in a class test is sixty per cent. If there are forty-two questions, how many must be answered correctly to pass?

9   What is zero point zero five multiplied by one thousand?

10   A school trip requires three forty-seater coaches to hold the pupils and teachers. Two of the coaches are full and the third is three-quarters full. How many teachers went on the trip if there was one teacher for every nine pupils?

11   A school wildlife pond is four metres in diameter. What is the diameter of the pond on a fifty to one scale drawing?

12   A school day ends at five past three. There are two lessons in the afternoon each lasting fifty minutes with a ten-minute break in between. At what time does the first afternoon lesson begin?

Chapter 2

General arithmetic

Maths audit 2

For the general arithmetic questions you need to know the following.

Decimal numbers

- How to round a decimal to the nearest whole number.
- How to shorten a decimal number to a given number of decimal places.

Measurement

- How to convert units of weight, length and volume in the metric system.
- How to work out the areas of basic shapes and borders.
- How to work out perimeters.
- How to read scales on maps.

Averages

- How to work out the arithmetic mean, median and modal value (mode).
- How to work out weighted averages.

Algebra

- How to work out arithmetic problems that contain brackets.

- How to solve problems that contain two or more arithmetic signs using the correct sequence of operations ('BIDMAS').

- How to work out simple formulae.

How to round decimal numbers – decimal place (d.p.)

Sometimes the numbers you obtain from a calculation are longer than is required for a sensible answer. For example:

$3.75 \times 4.01 = 15.0375$

If this level of *accuracy* is not required then you can shorten the number by *rounding it off*. To do this, you decrease the number of numbers to the right of the decimal point, ie you decrease the number of decimal places (d.p.).

For example, a number such as 15.0375 that has four decimal places (four numbers to the right of the decimal point) can be rounded off so that it has 3, 2 or 1 d.p.

Method:

If the *number to the right* of the decimal place you are shortening to is 5 *or more*, then you increase the number in the decimal place by 1; if is less than 5 it remains the same. For example:

Round off 15.0375 to three decimal places – ie 3 numbers to the right of the decimal point.

Answer: the number to the right of the third decimal place is 5 (15.037<u>5</u>) so we increase the number in the third decimal place by 1.

15.0375 becomes 15.038
15.0375 = 15.038 correct to 3 d.p.

Other examples are:

Round off 15.0375 to 2 decimal places
Answer: 15.0375 to 2 d.p. = 15.04

Round off 15.0375 to 1 decimal place
Answer: 15.0375 to 1 d.p. = 15.0

Round off 1.973 to 1 d.p.

more than 5 so the
9 becomes a 10 (making 1 unit)

Answer 1.973 to 1 d.p. = 2.0 (one decimal place showing)

Round off 1.973 to 2 d.p.

less than 5 so the
7 remains the same

Answer 1.973 to 2 d.p. = 1.97 (two decimal places showing)

1 *Warm-up exercise*

From the five alternatives (1, 2, 3, 4, or 5) choose *one* which completes the statement:

1 6.08323 to 2 d.p. is

6.083	6.08	6.0	6.0832	6.09
1	2	3	4	5

Answer

2 0.385426 to 5 d.p. is

0.38543	0.39	0.3854	0.385	0.4
1	2	3	4	5

Answer

3 0.754 to 1 d.p. is

0.75	0.7	0.754	0.8	1.0
1	2	3	4	5

Answer

4 7.956 to 2 d.p. is

7.95	8.0	7.96	7.9	7.956
1	2	3	4	5

Answer

2 Warm-up exercise

Work out the following and then *give your answer* to the number of decimal places shown:

1   25 ÷ 6   (to 2 d.p.)   *Answer* ....

2   100 ÷ 7   (to 4 d.p.)   *Answer* ....

3   3.45 × 3   (to 1 d.p.)   *Answer* ....

4   14.5 × 3   (to the nearest whole number = to 0 d.p.)

                                                         Answer ....

Work out the following and then give your answer to the nearest whole number:

5   325 ÷ 4   *Answer* ....

6   1279 ÷ 8   *Answer* ....

7   655 ÷ 10   *Answer* ....

8   100 ÷ 6   *Answer* ....

9   73 ÷ 22   *Answer* ....

10   400 ÷ 3   *Answer* ....

The metric system of measurement (SI units)

The most important metric measurements are weight, length and volume. SI units (international system) are in most cases the same as metric units, all being based on units of 10.

Weight

The basic unit of weight is the gram (g). All metric weights are based on this. There are three weights you are likely to encounter:

Name	Symbol
kilogram	kg
gram	g
milligram	mg

1 kg = 1000 g;   1 g = 1000 mg

Length

The basic unit of length is the metre (m). All metric lengths are based on this. There are four lengths you may encounter:

Name	Symbol
kilometre	km
metre	m
centimetre	cm
millimetre	mm

1 km = 1000 m; 1 m = 100 cm; 1 cm = 10 mm

Volume of liquids and gases (capacity)

Quantities of liquids and gases are measured in litres (l) and millilitres (ml) where 1 l = 1000 ml. You may also come across:

decilitre (dl) = one-tenth of a litre = 100 ml
centilitre (cl) = one-hundredth of a litre = 10 ml
cubic centimetre (cc or cm^3) = one-thousandth of a litre = 1 ml

Adding and subtracting metric units

When working out sums with metric units it is important that all the numbers have the same units. For example:

add 5 cm to 2 m, ie:
2 m + 5 cm = 2 m + 0.05 m = 2.05 m
1 g + 25 mg = 1 g + 0.025 g = 1.025 g
0.6 g − 500 mg = 600 mg − 500 mg = 100 mg or
0.6 g − 500 mg = 0.6 g − 0.5 g = 0.1 g

Areas, borders, perimeters and volumes

Areas

The metric units of area are square metre (m^2), square centimetre (cm^2) and square millimetre (mm^2).

Area of a square of side length $a = a \times a = a^2$.

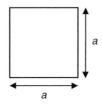

Area of a rectangle = length (l) × breadth (b) = $l \times b$.

The area of any triangle is found by multiplying half the base by the vertical height.

Area = ½ base × vertical height = ½ bh

Area of a circle of radius $r = \pi r^2$ (pi r squared). The diameter is twice as long as the radius, ie $d = 2r$ and $r = ½ d$. Substituting ½ d for r in πr^2 gives:

Area $= \pi \, (½ \, d)^2 = \pi \times ½ \, d \times ½ \, d = \pi \, ¼ \, d^2 = \pi \times \dfrac{d^2}{4}$

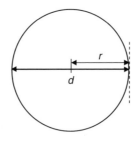

$\pi = 3.142$ (to 3 decimal places) or roughly $\dfrac{22}{7}$

Borders

The area of any border is given by the area of the outside shape minus area of the inside shape. For example:

Area of border = area outer rectangle − area inner rectangle
= 12 × 6 − 8 × 4
= 72 − 32 = 40 cm²

12 cm

6 cm   4 cm

8 cm

Perimeters

The perimeter of any shape is the distance all the way around the outside of the shape. Examples are:

Perimeter of a square = 4 × length of side

Perimeter of a rectangle = 2 × length × breadth

Perimeter of a circle = circumference: $c = 2\pi r = \pi d$

Volumes of solids

Volume is a measure of the space taken up by a three-dimensional object. It is measured in units cubed (units³) and the standard units of volume are the cubic metre (m³), cubic centimetre (cm³) and the cubic millimetre (mm³).

The most common solids have a prism shape, which means they have the same cross-section throughout their length.

10 cm

2 cm

6 cm

Volume = area of front face × length = 2 × 6 × 10 = 120 cm³

Scales

These are used when something very large is drawn in reduced form. Typical examples are maps and scale drawings of houses (blueprints). Scales are usually given in the form of a ratio of length (or distance) on the scale drawing to a length (or distance) of the real thing. Scales can vary enormously from, for example, one-sixth scale (eg house floor plans) to one fifty-thousandth scale (eg for maps).

Scales can be shown as either a fraction, eg ¼ or as a proportion, eg 1:4 (one to four) meaning that one unit of length on the drawing represents four units of length on the real thing. A map scale given as $\frac{1}{50000}$ or 1:50000 means that one unit of length on the map is equivalent to 50000 units on the ground, ie 1 cm on the map = 50000 cm on the ground = 500 m = 0.5 km. So 1 cm on the map equals 0.5 km on the ground (a '2 cm to 1 km' map). The most popular map scale is 1:25000 scale, which is the same as 1 cm: 0.25 km (a '4 cm to 1 km' map). Another way to show a map scale is to use a graphic, as shown below. Here the scale will remain true even if the size of the map is changed by photocopying.

Aspects of algebra

There are arithmetic rules for positively signed and negatively signed numbers. The following examples explain the correct procedures for combining signs:

$12 - 3 = 9$
$-12 - 3 = -15$
$-12 + 3 = -9$
$-12 \times 3 = -36$
$-12 \times -3 = 36$
$12 \div -3 = -4$
$-12 \div 3 = -4$
$-12 \div -3 = 4$
$-12 \times -3 \times -2 = -72$
$-12 \times -3 \times -2 \times -2 = 144$

Multiplication signs are omitted if brackets are used:

$(-12)(-3)(-2) = -72$, ie not $(-12) \times (-3) \times (-2) = -72$

Rearranging linear equations

Linear equations have letters with a power of one – there are no squared terms. Examples of linear equations can be found in mathematics, science and everyday life. Typical examples are:

temperature conversion;
speed, distance and time;
ratio and proportion;
maps and scales;
VAT and income tax; and
electrical power.

Examples of linear equations and algebraic manipulation are:

calculate distance travelled (D) from speed (S) and time (T):
$D = ST$ (and $T = D \div S$; $S = D \div T$)

calculate power in watts (W) from volts (V) and amps (A):
$W = VA$ (and $V = W \div A$; $A = W \div V$)

The following formula is more difficult to rearrange because it requires more than one step. In the test you will only be required to insert values into a formula to arrive at the answer. However, your ability to find solutions to problems will increase if you can move letters and numbers around easily from one side of an equation to the other.

To convert temperature from Fahrenheit to Celsius:

rearrange $F = \dfrac{9}{5}C + 32$ to leave C on its own:

i)   subtract 32 from both sides to give $F - 32 = \dfrac{9}{5}C + 0$

ii)   now multiply both sides by $\dfrac{5}{9}$ to give $\dfrac{5}{9}(F - 32) = \dfrac{5}{9} \times \dfrac{9}{5}C$

So $\dfrac{5}{9}(F - 32) = 1 \times C$, ie $C = \dfrac{5}{9}(F - 32)$

To convert Celsius to Fahrenheit:

rearrange $C = \dfrac{5}{9}(F - 32)$ to leave F on its own:

i)   multiply both sides by $\dfrac{9}{5}$ to give $\dfrac{9}{5}C = F - 32$ in a single step

ii)   add 32 to both sides to give $\dfrac{9}{5}C + 32 = F$, ie $F = \dfrac{9}{5}C + 32$;

(also $F = 1.8C + 32$ or $F = (C + 40) \times 1.8 - 40$)

Trends

You may be asked to spot a trend in a data series, typically an increase or decrease in a value with time; for example, school admissions over several years. In an *arithmetic series* there is a *common difference* between the numbers that enables you to predict the next number in the series. Examples include:

200	400	600	800		......?	(common difference = 200)
300	350	400	450		......?	(common difference = 50)
65	59	53	47	41	......?	(common difference = 6)
7.8	6.1	4.4	2.7		......?	(common difference = 1.7)

In another type of series the difference between consecutive numbers increases (or decreases) with each change, for example:

1	2	4	7	11	16	22	......?
+1	+2	+3	+4	+5	+6	+7	

In a *geometric series* the *ratio* of consecutive numbers is constant, for example, the numbers double or halve in value:

1 2 4 8 16 32 64 128 256 512 ......?
(common ratio = 2)

96	48	24	12	6	......?	(common ratio = 0.50)
20000	4000	800	160	32	......?	(common ratio = 0.2)

Averages

You might have a group of numbers (a data set) and wish to find a single number that best represents the group, ie a central value. The most common method is to calculate the arithmetic mean.

Mean

Add all the numbers together then divide the total by the number of numbers. For example:

What is the mean height of the following group of pupils: 1.55 m, 1.62 m, 1.57 m, 1.65 m and 1.51 m?

The mean is the sum total of the heights divided by five:

$$\frac{1.55 + 1.62 + 1.57 + 1.65 + 1.51}{5} = 7.9 \text{ m} \div 5 = 1.58 \text{ m}$$

Alternatives to the mean are the median and mode.

Median

The median is the middle number in a group of numbers that have been placed in numerical order, from smallest to the largest. From the previous example:

1st	2nd	3rd	4th	5th
1.51	1.55	1.57	1.62	1.65

The median is given by the middle value, which in this case is the third number, ie 1.57 m.

Here is another example. What is the median average of the following numbers?

4.3   10   3   7.5   5   9   6.7   5

Step 1: rearrange in ascending order, repeating any numbers where necessary:

3   4.3   5   5   6.7   7.5   9   10

There is an even number of numbers in this group and, therefore, no 'middle value' as such.

Step 2: to find the 'middle value' you work out the mean of the two middle numbers:

$5 + 6.7 = 11.7 \div 2 = 5.85$ = median of the group.

To locate the middle position of a large group of numbers (n), add 1 and divide by 2, ie (n + 1) ÷ 2. For example:

You have 51 numbers. The middle position (median) is found by adding 1 and dividing by 2: (51 + 1) ÷ 2 = 26th number.

You have 50 numbers. The middle position is found by adding 1 and dividing by 2: (50 + 1) ÷ 2 = 25.5 so you have to average the 25th and 26th numbers to find the median.

Mode

The mode is the value that occurs most often.

For example, in this group of numbers – 3 4 7 3 4 5 3 9 8 6 3 – the mode (modal value) is 3 because it occurs most frequently – four times. If two values are equally popular then the group is said to be 'bi-modal'. For example, in the group 5 5 7 8 3 7 4 1 2, the modal values are 5 and 7.

If more than two numbers occur equally most frequently in a group then the mode would not be used as a way of expressing the average value.

Range

The range measures the spread of the data, ie the maximum value minus the minimum value. For example:

5 5 7 8 3 7 4 1 2 – range = 8 – 1 = 7

Weighted average

In a weighted average test, some scores count more than others towards the overall result. Weighted averages are used in coursework and in university degree classification. Examples of degree course weighting are:

1:3:5	first year = 1/9; second year = 3/9; final year = 5/9
1:3	second year = 25%; final year = 75%
1:2	second year = 0.33; final year = 0.67

The weighted average is calculated as follows:

i) convert each mark or score to its percentage (eg 16 correct answers out of 20 marks = 80%);

ii) multiply each percentage mark by its weight (expressed as either a fraction, percentage or decimal);

iii) sum the results, giving your answer as a percentage.

The following equations show you how to work out the weighted average of the three examples given above:

1:3:5	Overall mark = (1 × Yr1 % + 3 × Yr2 % + 5 × Yr3 %) ÷ 9
1:3	Overall mark = Yr2 % × 25% + Yr3 % × 75%
1:2	Overall mark = Yr2 × 0.33 + Yr3 × 0.67

If you are not given an equation then you need to multiply each percentage mark by its percentage weight and add the results together. For example:

A student scores 16 out of 20 in Test 1 and 32 out of 50 in Test 2. If the tests are weighted 25% for Test 1 and 75% for Test 2, what is the overall percentage?

Step i)   16/20 = 80%; 32/50 = 64%

Step ii) $80 \times 25\% = 20$; $64 \times 75\% = 48$

Step iii)   20 + 48 = 68%

3 Warm-up exercise

Work out the average of the following groups of numbers:

1   2, 3, 4   *Answer* ....

2   9, 7, 2, 6, 1   *Answer* ....

3   20, 30, 40   *Answer* ....

4   47, 3, 22, 8, 16, 6   *Answer* ....

5   100, 110, 120, 130   *Answer* ....

4 Warm-up exercise

Find the modal value:

1   12, 10, 14, 15, 11, 9, 7, 14, 13   *Answer* ....

2   1, 2, 1, 1, 4, 3, 2, 2, 3, 1, 3, 1, 3, 2   *Answer* ....

Find the median:

3   12, 10, 14, 15, 11, 9, 7, 14, 13   *Answer* ....

4   12, 10, 14, 15, 11, 9, 7, 14   *Answer* ....

Find the range:

5   12, 10, 14, 15, 11, 9, 7, 14, 13   *Answer* ....

5 Easy questions

1   If the average of the following set of numbers is 6, what is the value of x?

3, 10, x, 5, 8   *Answer* ....

2   If the average of the following set of numbers is 16, what is the value of y?

20, y, 13, 15, 9, 22, 17, 11   *Answer* ....

3   If the mean average of the following numbers is 8, what is the mode if x is a positive integer?

7, 10, 8, x, 9, 8, 6, 10, 7   *Answer* ....

4   In the following set of numbers the mean is 5. What is the median if x is a positive integer?

7, 3, 5, 8, 7, x, 4, 4, 6, 8, 2, 2, 8   *Answer* ....

5   In an evaluation test, scores ranged from 1 to 5 as shown in the table below. What is the mean score?

Score	Frequency
1	5
2	1
3	3
4	1
5	0

Answer ....

6   A class of 25 pupils were asked how many siblings they had. The results are shown in the table below.

Siblings	1	1	2	3	4
Number of pupils	7	8	6	3	1

Calculate:

a)   the mean number of siblings;   *Answer* ....

b)   the modal number of siblings;   *Answer* ....

c)   the median number of siblings.   *Answer* ....

Chapter 3

Statistics

Maths audit 3

For the statistical questions you need to know the following:

- *Pie charts*: how to read data from a pie chart (multiply the total by the fraction shown).
- *Bar charts*: how to read data off a bar chart (read across to the vertical axis from the top of each bar).
- *Line graphs*: how to read data points on a line graph (read values off the horizontal and vertical axes).
- *Histograms*: how to read histograms created from tally charts and frequency tables.
- *Cumulative frequency graphs*: how to find the median, the upper quartile, the lower quartile; how many were below a given mark and how many were above a given grade.
- *Box and whisker plots*: how to use a box and whisker plot to identify six key pieces of information.
- *Tables*: how to locate information in tables and how to read two-way tables.

Most of the QTS numeracy questions in the 'on-screen' section involve charts, graphs or tables; they provide a simple and efficient way of displaying school data. You can expect to see a few easy questions, or 'one-liners' where the answer can be read directly from a chart or table. However, the majority of the answers require a careful interpretation of the question to locate the data, followed by the application of mathematical operations.

You are not expected to solve every problem in your head, in which case you will find it helpful to jot down a few numbers as you go along. If you need to use a calculator it is useful to have a rough idea of the size of the answer first. This book will not teach you how or when to use a calculator; you are expected to be able to key in the appropriate figures. Thus to work out 20% of 160,000 (see Figure 3.3) you would enter: $20 \div 100 \times 160,000 =$. Alternatively you could short-cut this to $0.2 \times 160,000$ or go one step further and work it out mentally as $2 \times 16,000$.

Pie charts

These charts are not the most accurate way of displaying data but they do show at a glance the relative sizes of component parts. A full circle (360°) represents 100 per cent of the data, so 180° = one-half (50%), 120° = one-third (33.3%) and 90° = one-quarter (25%), etc. Reading information from pie charts is easy, but marks are lost when the candidate fails to look at the text in a key or sub-heading.

Now attempt the single-step questions associated with the two pie charts in Figures 3.1 and 3.2, for which a calculator is not required. You will need to use a calculator to answer some of the questions based on the single pie chart in Figure 3.3.

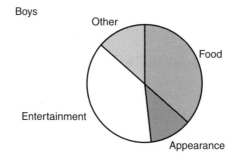

FIGURE 3.1   Distribution of boys' expenditure aged 7 to 15

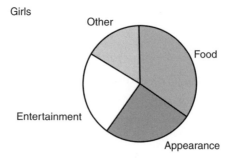

FIGURE 3.2   Distribution of girls' expenditure aged 7 to 15

1 *Warm-up exercise*

1   What is the most popular area of girls' spending?

2   What is the least popular area of boys' spending?

3   In which area do boys and girls spend a similar proportion of their money?

4   What percentage of girls' spending is taken up by appearance (quarter circle)?

5   Girls spend twice as much as boys on appearance. What fraction of boys' expenditure is taken up by appearance?

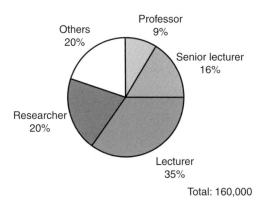

Total: 160,000

FIGURE 3.3   Grade of staff in higher education institutions

2 *Warm-up exercise*

1   What percentage of the staff are researchers?

2   What fraction of the staff are researchers?

3   What fraction of the staff are lecturer grade?

4   What fraction of the staff are senior lecturer grade?

5   What is the combined total of lecturers and senior lecturers as a decimal fraction of the whole?

6   How many staff are researchers?

7   How many more senior lecturers and researchers combined are there than lecturers?

8   How many staff are professors?

9   If there are five times as many male professors as female professors, how many female professors are there?

Bar charts

Bar graphs (bar charts) are useful for comparing different categories of data, for example GCSE subjects, or school results in different years. The bars can be drawn vertically or horizontally. The height (or length) of each bar is read off the scale on the axis and corresponds to the size of the data.

The bar graph in Figure 3.4 shows a school's seven most popular GCSE subjects.

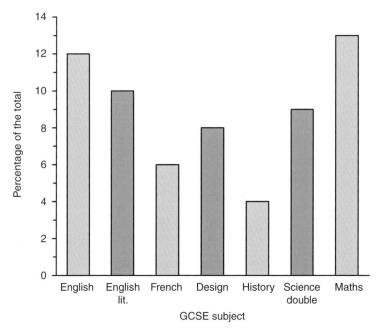

FIGURE 3.4 School subject by popularity

3 Warm-up exercise

1 Which subject is the most popular?

2 Which subject is the fifth most popular?

3 Which subject is three times more popular than History?

4 Which subject is two-thirds as popular as Science double?

5 What proportion of the total is taken up by English Literature? Give your answer as a fraction in its lowest terms and also as a decimal.

6 What proportion of the total is taken up by English and Maths together? Give your answer as a fraction in its lowest terms.

7 What is the ratio of pupils taking English literature to pupils taking English? Give your answer in its lowest terms.

8 If 180 pupils take English, how many take English literature?

9 What percentage of the total is taken up by all seven subjects?

10 What decimal fraction of the total is taken up by subjects other than those shown in the chart?

The bar chart in Figure 3.5 shows the percentage of pupils achieving grades A* to C in five popular subjects.

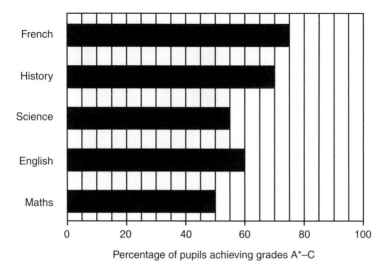

Percentage of pupils achieving grades A*–C

FIGURE 3.5 Bar chart of grades achieved in five subjects

4 Easy questions

1 If 180 pupils took GCSE Maths, how many achieved grades A* to C?

2 One-third as many pupils took History as took Maths. How many pupils achieved grades A* to C in History?

3 If English and Maths were equally popular, how many more pupils gained grades A* to C in English than in Maths?

4 If 54 pupils achieved grades A* to C in French, how many pupils took French?

In a stacked (compound) bar chart each bar is split into two or more segments that represent different data sets. The data are easier to compare than would be the case if the segments were shown as individual bars placed side by side. The stacked bar chart in Figure 3.6 compares pupils at Key Stage 2 achieving levels 2 to 5 in Maths in two schools, A and B.

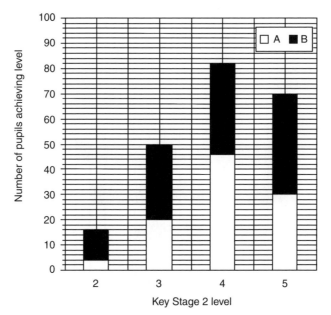

FIGURE 3.6   Stacked bar chart showing performance at Key Stage 2

5 Easy questions

1   At which level did school A outperform school B?

2   The graph shows that the number of pupils achieving level 2 at school B was three times that of school A (3:1 ratio). What was the B:A ratio for pupils achieving level 3?

Line graphs

With these graphs the data are plotted as a series of points joined by a line. Figure 3.7 shows a travel graph where the distance travelled in miles is plotted against the time in hours. The controlling quantity (time) is plotted on the x-axis and the quantity it controls (distance travelled) is plotted on the y-axis. The data table for the graph is shown in Table 3.1.

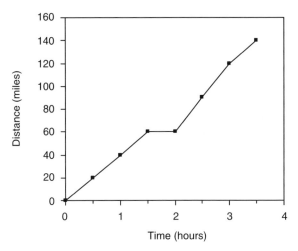

FIGURE 3.7   Distance–time graph for a school coach

TABLE 3.1   Distance–time data table for a school coach

Time (hours)	0	0.5	1.0	1.5	2.0	2.5	3.0	3.5
Dist. (miles)	0	20	40	60	60	90	120	140

6 Easy questions

1   What was the average speed for the journey?

2   For how many minutes was the coach stationary?

3   If the coach set out at 1000 hrs, what was the average speed between midday and 1330 hrs, to the nearest mile per hour?

4   What are the x and y coordinates of the point at 1300 hrs?

Multiple line graphs

Line graphs are useful for showing trends. Two or more lines can be shown together on the same axes to facilitate comparisons. The line graph in Figure 3.8 compares a local authority's A-level passes in Maths, Physics, Chemistry and Biology.

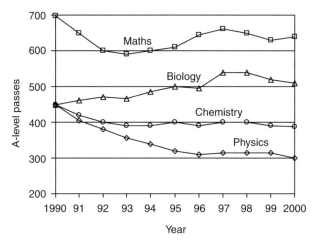

FIGURE 3.8   A-level passes for a local authority

7 Easy questions

1   Which subject showed the least variation in passes from 1990 to 2000 (least change)?

2   What was the range of the passes for Physics between 1990 and 2000 (maximum minus minimum)?

3   In 1995, how many more passes were there in Biology than in Chemistry?

4   Assuming the rate of decline in Maths passes from 1990 to 1992 had continued, how many Maths passes would have been predicted for the year 2000 (extend the line downwards or calculate the common difference)?

The graph in Figure 3.9 shows the percentage of pupils in a school achieving levels 5 to 8 and levels 3 to 8 in Maths at Key Stage 3.

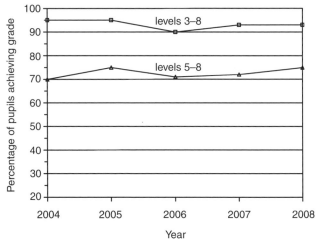

FIGURE 3.9   Pupil achievement at Key Stage 3 Maths

8 Easy questions

1   What percentage of the pupils achieved levels 5 to 8 in 2004?

2   What percentage of the pupils achieved less than level 5 in 2004? (Hint: level 3–8 = 3, 4, 5, 6, 7, 8; level 5–8 = 5, 6, 7, 8.)

3   What fraction of the pupils achieved levels 5 to 8 in 2005? Give your answer in its lowest terms.

4   What fraction of the pupils achieved less than level 5 in 2005? (Hint: level 3–8 = 3, 4, 5, 6, 7, 8; level 5–8 = 5, 6, 7, 8.)

Scatter graphs

These are similar to line graphs in that points are plotted and a line can be drawn. However, the line is not drawn from point to point but is a 'line of best fit' through all of the points. This 'regression line' can be judged by eye or it can be calculated. The line identifies any relationship (correlation) between the x and y values, as shown in the following examples:

a) Strong positive correlation; points lie close to a straight line (*x* and *y* increase in proportion to each other).

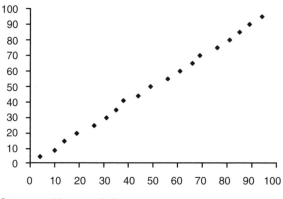

FIGURE 3.10   Strong positive correlation

b) Weak positive correlation; points are not close to a line.

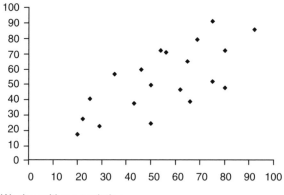

FIGURE 3.11   Weak positive correlation

c) No correlation; random (unable to predict *x* from *y*).

FIGURE 3.12   No correlation

Figure 3.13 is a scatter graph showing a strong negative correlation between Key Stage 2 performance and pupil absenteeism.

FIGURE 3.13   Strong negative correlation

9 *More difficult questions*

1   What percentage of pupils would be expected to achieve level 4+ if they had 23 half-days of absence?

2   Pupils in a school have on average 10 days of absence each. If 70% achieve level 4 or above, is this better or worse than expected?

3   Pupils in a school have on average 8 days of absence each. If 90% achieve level 4 or above, is this better or worse than expected?

Figure 3.14 shows a scatter graph comparing results in an arithmetic test with results in a writing test.

FIGURE 3.14   Scatter graph of arithmetic and writing test results

10 *More difficult questions*

Use the three dashed lines to help you to determine:

1   Which pupil did equally well in both tests?

2   How many pupils did better in writing than in arithmetic?

3   How many pupils did better in arithmetic than in writing?

4   How many pupils gained 10 or more marks in arithmetic?

5   How many pupils gained 10 or more marks in writing?

6   How many pupils gained 10 or more marks in both writing and arithmetic?

7   How many pupils gained 10 or fewer marks in both writing and arithmetic?

8   Which pupil had the largest difference in arithmetic and writing test results?

Tables

Here you are given a table of data followed by one or more questions. You need to look along a row and down a column to find the answer. Table 3.2 has 8 columns and 10 rows.

11 Warm-up exercise

Table 3.2 shows temperatures in degrees Celsius (°C) of holiday resorts in Switzerland, from April to October.

TABLE 3.2 Temperature versus resort

	Apr	May	Jun	Jul	Aug	Sep	Oct
Interlaken	11	15	19	21	21	17	12
Adelboden	8	13	14	16	19	17	10
Central Reg.	12	17	20	22	21	17	12
Lake Geneva	11	16	19	22	21	17	13
Zermatt	8	13	17	19	19	16	10
Verbier	14	19	22	24	23	19	14
Davos	6	11	14	16	16	13	7
St Moritz	1	6	9	11	10	5	1
Lake Lugano	14	19	23	26	26	22	16

With reference to the table:

1 Which is the coldest resort?   *Answer* ....

2 Which is the warmest month for most of the resorts?   *Answer* ....

3 Which two resorts have the same highest temperature in June?
                                                             Answer ....

4 In which month are four of the resorts at the same temperature?
                                                             Answer ....

5 How many resorts achieved 20 °C or more in July?   *Answer* ....

6 In how many resorts does the temperature drop below 10 °C?
                                                             Answer ....

7 In how many resorts does the temperature rise above 10 °C?
                                                             Answer ....

8   What is the difference in temperature between Interlaken and St Moritz in July?

Answer ....

9   Which resort shows the largest increase in temperature, April to July?

Answer ....

10   In which month is Davos four degrees cooler than Lake Geneva?

Answer ....

11   What is the average temperature in Verbier for June, July and August?

Answer ....

12   What is the average temperature in St Moritz for all seven months?

Answer ....

13   What is the average temperature of all the resorts in October?

Answer ....

14   Which resort has the highest 'mean' (ie average) temperature over the seven months? (Hint: no calculation necessary)   Answer ....

15   Which resort offers the least variation (ie change) in temperature between May and July?   Answer ....

16   What is the range of temperature (ie highest minus lowest) in Zermatt over the seven months?   Answer ....

12 Easy questions

TABLE 3.3   Points score versus GCSE grade (old system)

GCSE Grade	Points
A*	8
A	7
B	6
C	5
D	4
E	3
F	2
G	1

Example:
Pupil with 8 GCSEs
2 A grades = 2 × 7 = 14 points
3 B grades = 3 × 6 = 18 points
2 C grades = 2 × 5 = 10 points
1 D = 4 points
Total = 46 points
Average score = 46 ÷ 8 = 5.75

1   What is the total score for a pupil with an A grade in English, B grades in Sociology and Psychology, and C grades in Maths, History and Economics?

2   What is the average points score for the pupil in question 1? Give your answer to two decimal places.

Table 3.4 looks very different but presents similar data in the form of eight columns and two rows.

13 More difficult questions

TABLE 3.4   Points score versus GCSE grade (new system)

Grade	G	F	E	D	C	B	A	A*
Points	16	22	28	34	40	46	52	58

A school can predict a pupil's GCSE grade in core subjects based on the level achieved at Key Stage 3 using the formula:

Point score = 6 × KS3 level + 3

1   How many points would be expected for a pupil with a level 7 in Maths at Key Stage 3?

2   What would be the most likely GCSE grade for the pupil in question 1?

3   A pupil gains a level 5 in English at Key Stage 3. What GCSE grade would be predicted?

4   A pupil is awarded GCSE grade B in Science. What level would you have expected at Key Stage 3?

5   A pupil gained level 7 in English and Science and level 6 in Maths. What were the pupil's average points?

6   What are the total points for a pupil achieving level 7 in eight subjects?

7   What are the average points for a pupil with two Bs, four Cs and two Ds?

8   A pupil has a total of 8 GCSEs, including five Cs and two Bs. If the points totalled 314, what was the other grade?

Two-way tables

These are useful for comparing pupil performance in two subjects (or in two different years). One subject occupies the columns and the other subject occupies the rows. The cells show the number of times the subjects are paired at each grade or level; all the combinations possible can be recorded. The table may also include the total number (summation) of the combinations across each row and column.

Table 3.5 compares the GCSE results of pupils who took both French (vertical column) and Spanish (horizontal row). Where a cell is empty the number of pupils obtaining that combination of grades is zero.

TABLE 3.5   Two-way table for GCSE French and Spanish

GCSE grade in Spanish	GCSE grade in French								
	A*	A	B	C	D	E	F	G	Total
A*	1	2	1						4
A	1	2	1	1					5
B	1	2	3	2	1				9
C		1	2	4	2				9
D				2	1	1	1		5
E					1	1		1	3
F									0
G									0
Total	3	7	7	9	5	2	1	1	35

14 More difficult questions

1   How many pupils achieved a grade C in both French and Spanish?

2   How many pupils gained a grade C in Spanish?

3   How many pupils achieved a grade A in French?

4   How many pupils in total took both French and Spanish?

5   What was the modal grade for French?

6   How many pupils achieved grade C or above in Spanish?

7   What percentage of pupils achieved grade C or above in Spanish? (Give your answer to 1 decimal place.)

8   How many pupils achieved a lower grade in Spanish than in French (those left of a diagonal line from A*A* to GG)?

Tally charts, frequency tables and histograms

A tally chart is used to group and count data. The results are presented in a frequency table, and a frequency histogram (a bar chart of frequency distributions) is drawn. The histogram provides a mental picture of the spread of the marks with the most frequent marks normally centred on the middle. For example, 51 pupils achieved the following GCSE grades:

B C D E A B D C B A C C D C A* C E B A C B D C B C E D F D B C D B C D C F E C D B C D C D B C D C C B

The tally chart, frequency table and histogram are shown in Figure 3.15.

Tally chart

A*	I	1
A	III	3
B	~~HHT~~ ~~HHT~~ I	11
C	~~HHT~~ ~~HHT~~ ~~HHT~~ III	18
D	~~HHT~~ ~~HHT~~ II	12
E	IIII	4
F	II	2

Frequency table

Grade	F	E	D	C	B	A	A*
Frequency	2	4	12	18	11	3	1

Histogram

FIGURE 3.15   Tally chart, frequency table and histogram

The performance of a school can be assessed by allocating points to GCSE grades as described earlier and shown in Table 3.6. The frequency of the grades enables the total number of points to be calculated (points multiplied by frequency for every grade).

The mean value of all the points in the table is given by the total number of points divided by the total number of frequencies (total number of pupils):

TABLE 3.6   Allocating points to GCSE grades

Grade	F	E	D	C	B	A	A*
GCSE points	22	28	34	40	46	52	58
Frequency	2	4	12	18	11	3	1

$$\text{mean} = \frac{\text{'total of' [points multiplied by frequencies]}}{\text{'total number of frequencies'}}$$

$$= \frac{(58\times1)+(52\times3)+(46\times11)+(40\times18)+(34\times12)+(28\times4)+(22\times2)}{1+3+11+18+12+4+2}$$

$$= \frac{58+156+506+720+408+112+44}{51}$$

$$= 2004 \div 51 = 39.29 \text{ points}$$

The mean points per pupil are 39.29 or just below grade C (40).

The median points are those of the 26th pupil (middle of 51 is given by (n + 1) ÷ 2 = 52 ÷ 2 = 26th), found in the grade C group, ie median = 40 points. The modal points = 40 (most frequent points, 18 times).

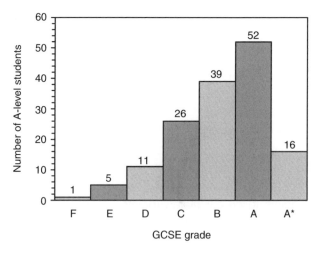

FIGURE 3.16   Histogram of GCSE grades for A-level students

15 More difficult questions

1   How many students achieved GCSE grades A* to F?

2   What percentage of the A*–F students achieved grade C or above? (Give your answer to 1 decimal place.)

3   What is the modal GCSE grade?

4   What is the median GCSE grade?

5   If 96% of the A-level students went on to higher education, how many students was this?

Histograms often group the marks into intervals, for example 10–19, 20–29, 30–39, etc to provide a clearer picture of the distribution of the marks; the bars should be touching because the data intervals are continuous.

The intervals can be described using the less than (<) and less than or equal to (≤) symbols to identify the boundaries of the marks:

symbol:	$n \le 9$	$9 < n \le 19$	$19 < n \le 29$	$29 < n \le 39$
interval:	0–9	10–19	20–29	30–39

Example: A sixth-form college converted the GCSE grades of 125 students to points. The points were averaged for each student to obtain a mean GCSE score (X); as shown in Table 3.7 and Figure 3.17.

TABLE 3.7   Example of intervals

Mean GCSE score (X)	Frequency
$4.5 < X \le 5.0$	5
$5.0 < X \le 5.5$	13
$5.5 < X \le 6.0$	27
$6.0 < X \le 6.5$	43
$6.5 < X \le 7.0$	25
$7.0 < X \le 7.5$	8
$7.5 < X \le 8.0$	4

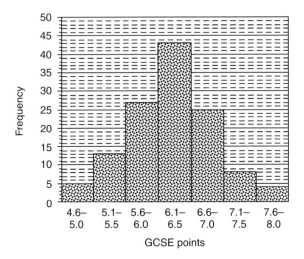

FIGURE 3.17   Histogram of GCSE points scores

16 *More difficult questions*

1   What percentage of the students scored more than 6 points?

2   What is the ratio of students scoring more than 6 points to students scoring 6 points or less?

3   What percentage of the students scored in the range shown by 5.5 < X ≤ 7.0?

Cumulative frequency graphs

These are S-shaped graphs that show how many pupils achieved a particular grade and below. The running total of frequencies (not the actual frequency) is plotted against the grade. The final running total always equals the total number of pupils; as shown in Table 3.8.

TABLE 3.8   Cumulative frequency table

Grade	F	E	D	C	B	A	A*
Frequency	2	3	12	18	11	4	1
Cumulative frequency	2	5	17	35	46	50	51
	2	2+3	5+12	17+18	35+11	46+4	50+1

FIGURE 3.18   Cumulative frequency graph of GCSE grades

17 More difficult questions

How many pupils achieved:

1   Grade C and below (ie up to grade C)?

2   Grade B and below (ie up to grade B)?

3   Grade A and below (ie up to grade A)?

There were 51 pupils in total. Refer to your answers in 1, 2 and 3 respectively to answer questions 4, 5 and 6.

How many pupils achieved:

4   Grade B and above? (Hint: 51 minus C and below)

5   Grade A and above? (Hint: 51 minus B and below)

6   Grade A*? (Hint: 51 minus A and below)

7   Grade C or above? (Hint: 51 minus grade D and below; or read from the table 18 + 11 + 4 + 1.)

8   Grade D or above?

9   What fraction of the pupils achieved grade C or above?

10   What percentage of the pupils achieved grade D or above? (Give your answer to 1 decimal place.)

11   What proportion of the pupils achieved grade B and above? (Give your answer to 1 decimal place.)

In the cumulative frequency graph in Figure 3.19 the GCSE grades have been converted to points, as shown in Table 3.9.

FIGURE 3.19   Cumulative frequency graph of GCSE points

TABLE 3.9   Cumulative frequency table

Grade	F	E	D	C	B	A	A*
GCSE points	22	28	34	40	46	52	58
Frequency	1	2	9	26	42	60	20
Cumulative frequency	1	3	12	38	80	140	160

The median is the points score of the middle student (80th) located half-way up the cumulative frequency axis.

18 More difficult questions

1   What is the highest GCSE points score?

2   What is the lowest GCSE points score?

3   What is the range of the GCSE points scores?

4   What is the median GCSE points score?

5   How many students achieved 52 points and below?

6   How many students achieved more than 52 points?

7   How many students achieved more than 34 points? (Read the *y*-axis scale carefully.)

One hundred students took a QTS numeracy test. The cumulative frequency graph in Figure 3.20 shows the percentage of pupils achieving a given mark or less.

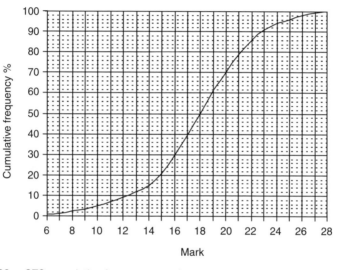

FIGURE 3.20   QTS cumulative frequency graph

19 *More difficult questions*

1   The median mark can be read from the 50th percentile* (50% cumulative frequency). What mark does this correspond to?

2   Which mark did 70% of the students fall below?

3   Which mark did 12% of the students fall below?

4   How many students achieved 16 marks or lower?

5   The pass mark is 17 out of 28. How many students passed?

* Percentiles: dividing the data (marks) into 100 equal parts.

Box and whisker plots

These plots provide a method of visualizing several key pieces of statistical information including the maximum and minimum values, the median and the spread (distribution) of the values.

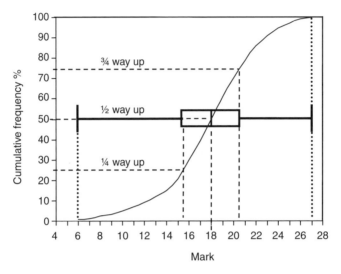

FIGURE 3.21 A box and whisker plot

Figure 3.21 shows a box and whisker plot drawn on the cumulative frequency chart shown in Figure 3.20.

The box and whisker plot summarizes seven key values based on splitting the data into four quarters, as shown in Figure 3.22.

FIGURE 3.22 Splitting the data into four quarters

6: the lowest mark (end of whisker);
15.5: the lower quartile mark at the 25th percentile;
18: the median mark at the 50th percentile;
20.5: the upper quartile mark at the 75th percentile;
27: highest mark (end of whisker);
20.5–15.5: the interquartile range;
27–6: the range (end of one whisker to the end of the other).

Box and whisker plots can also be drawn vertically, as shown in Figure 3.23. The plots compare pupil performance in three subjects.

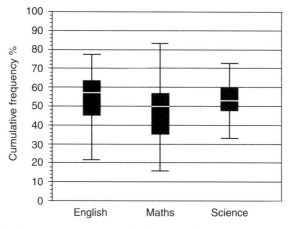

FIGURE 3.23   Vertical box and whisker plot for key subject exam results

The following points should be considered when answering the questions:

● The lower quartile is the mark below which one-quarter of the marks lie (it is the bottom 25% of the range) and three-quarters of the marks lie above it.

● The upper quartile is the mark above which one-quarter of the marks lie (it is the top 25% of the range) and three-quarters of the marks lie below it.

● The spread of the first and last quarters is shown by the length of the two whiskers drawn to the end points (the lowest mark and the highest mark).

● The spread of the two middle quarters is shown by the two boxes (each plot has two boxes and two whiskers) and represents the inter-quartile range.

● Half of the marks (50%) fall into the inter-quartile range.

20 *More difficult questions*

1   Which subject had the lowest mark?

2   Which subject had the highest median mark?

3   Which subject had the smallest inter-quartile range?

4   In which subject was the range of marks the highest?

5   In which subject did half the marks lie above 54% and half the marks lie below 54%?

6 Which subject had a similar number of marks in the upper and lower quartiles?

7 Above what mark did one-quarter of the Science marks lie?

8 Which subject had the widest range of marks for the top 25%?

9 If 80 pupils took the English test, how many were in the inter-quartile range?

10 Which subject had the highest proportion of pupils achieving 60% or more of the marks?

Introduction to the 'on-screen'-type mock tests

In the second section of the test, the questions appear on the screen. The following points are worth noting for the actual QTS test:

● Remember to use the on-screen calculator.

● Scroll forwards using the 'next' button and backwards using the 'previous' button to find the easier questions; plan to skip the more difficult questions, leaving them until the end of the test.

● Do not accidentally click on the 'end exam' button.

● The 'exhibit' button displays additional information.

● The clock shows the time remaining.

● There is no need to include units with your answers.

● The mouse is used for 'drag and drop' and 'point and click' answers.

● There is more time than you might think, so do not rush.

There now follow two mock 'on-screen' tests of 16 questions each. You have 35 minutes to complete each test, or just over two minutes per question. If you find any question difficult, skip it and return to it later. Make sure that you have a calculator to hand as well as a pen and paper.

Some questions will ask you to 'indicate all the true statements', in which case you tick the correct answer(s), or mark the statements True (T) or False (F), as per the answers at the end of the book. In the actual test you have to click inside a box to bring up a tick mark alongside the correct answer(s).

Mock test 1
(16 'on-screen' questions in 35 minutes)

Question 1

Temperatures in Celsius (C) can be converted to temperatures in Fahrenheit (F) using the following formula:

$F = ((C+40) \times 1.8) - 40$

What is 20°C converted to Fahrenheit?

Answer

Question 2

A teacher summarized the marks in a Maths test using the box and whisker plot below.

22   38   43   54   72

Indicate all the true statements:

1   At least one pupil achieved 72 marks.

Answer

2   The interquartile range was 16.

Answer

3   One-quarter of the pupils scored more than 38 marks.

Answer

Question 3

The following table compares a school's A-level entries in Chemistry, Physics and Biology according to sex.

	Chemistry	Physics	Biology
Boys	36	45	30
Girls	32	10	50

Indicate all the true statements:

1   The ratio of boys to girls in Chemistry was 8:9.

Answer _____

2   The ratio of girls to boys in Physics was 2:9.

Answer _____

3   The ratio of boys to girls in Biology was 5:3.

Answer _____

Question 4

The graph shows the cumulative frequency of a school's SPaG test results.

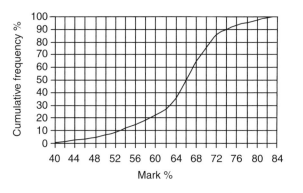

Indicate all the true statements:

1   The median mark was 50%.

Answer _____

2   The upper quartile is at about 70% of the marks.

Answer _____

3   At least 90% of the pupils achieved a mark above 50%.

Answer _____

Question 5

The table shows a school's GCSE grade distribution in core subjects.

	Maths	English	Science
A*–C	89%	92%	95%
A*–G	96%	100%	98%

Indicate all the true statements:

1   11% of Maths pupils failed to achieve a grade C or above.

Answer ⬚

2   The number of pupils achieving grade A*–C in Science was higher than the number achieving grades A*–C in English.

Answer ⬚

3   Two out of every 25 English grades were D, E, F or G.

Answer ⬚

Question 6
On a school trip to Paris a teacher runs out of Euros. She exchanges £200 for Euros at an exchange rate of 13 Euros for every £10. The teacher spends 195 Euros and at the end of the trip exchanges the remaining Euros back into pounds at the same exchange rate. How many pounds does she have?

Answer ⬚

Question 7
The pie charts show the distribution of A-level grades in two different schools, A and B.

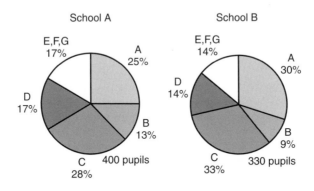

Indicate all the true statements:

1   School B achieved more A grades than School A.

Answer ⬚

2   The number of pupils achieving grade C or above in School A was 264.

Answer ⬚

3   The A–C pass rate in School B was 6% above that in School A.

Answer ⬚

Question 8

The table shows the percentage of pupils achieving Level 4 and above at Key Stage 2 English, Maths and Science between 2001 and 2005.

	Pupils achieving level 4+ at Key Stage 2 (%)		
Year	English	Maths	Science
2001	75	71	87
2002	75	73	86
2003	75		87
2004	77	74	86
2005	79	75	86
Mean		73.2	86.4

Indicate all the true statements:

1   The mean for English for the five-year period was 76.2%.

Answer [   ]

2   72% of Maths pupils achieved level 4 or above in 2003.

Answer [   ]

3   For science for the five-year period the mode was 86% and the median was 86.5%.

Answer [   ]

Question 9

The table shows test scores in reading, writing and arithmetic.

	Reading score (out of 40)	Writing score (out of 50)	Arithmetic score (out of 60)
Lowest	15	18	25
Median	29	36	47
Highest	36	43	54

Which test had the highest percentage mark and the smallest range?

Answer [   ]

Question 10

Photocopying paper weighs 80 g/m². The dimensions of a single sheet are 21 cm × 30 cm. What is the weight of a five-ream box of paper, in kilograms? (1 ream = 500 sheets.)

Answer [   ]

Question 11

The bar chart shows Key Stage 2 level 4+ performance in English versus the proportion of pupils eligible for free school meals in an LEA's schools for 2000 and 2004.

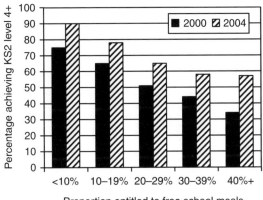

Indicate all the true statements:

1   The percentage of pupils achieving KS2 level 4+ in English in 2004 was above that for 2000.

Answer [   ]

2   The schools with the highest proportion of pupils on free school meals showed the greatest improvements in KS2 performance from 2000 to 2004.

Answer [   ]

3   In 2004, less than 10% of the pupils achieved KS2 level 4+ in schools where 90% were entitled to free school meals.

Answer [   ]

Question 12

The table shows pupil performance at the end of Key Stage 3 English, Maths and Science.

Name	English KS3 level	Maths KS3 level	Science KS3 level
Aziz	6	5	5
Bethan	5	4	5
Carl	5	5	6
Eleri	4	6	4
Harry	5	5	6
Josh	5	4	5
Phoebe	7	7	7
Ruby	5	5	6
Yasmin	4	4	5
Zak	6	6	5
% at level 5 or above		70	90
% at level 6 or above	50	60	30

1   What percentage of the pupils achieved level 5 or above in English?

Answer [   ]

2   What proportion of the pupils who achieved level 5 or above in Science also achieved level 5 or above in Maths? Give your answer as a fraction in its lowest terms.

Answer [   ]

3   What proportion of the pupils achieved level 5 or above in all three subjects? Give your answer as a percentage.

Answer [   ]

Question 13

Pupils are taken on a field trip to Ireland via the Holyhead–Dublin ferry. The ferry timetable is shown below.

	Holyhead to Dublin		Dublin to Holyhead	
Vessel	Departs	Arrives	Departs	Arrives
Cruise	0240	0555	0805	1130
Swift	1200	1355	0845	1045
Cruise	1410	1525	1430	1630
Swift	1715	1915	2055	0020
	Latest check-in time is 30 minutes before departure

What is the latest check-in time if the pupils are to arrive back in Holyhead before midday?

Answer [   ]

Question 14

The graph shows the percentage of pupils at Key Stage 1 Maths level 3 from 2002 to 2007 for a school and its local authority.

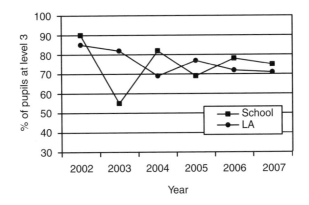

In which year did the school's performance exceed that of the local authority by more than 10%?

Answer [   ]

Question 15

A pupil sat four tests, namely Test 1A, Test 1B, Test 2A and Test 2B. The test results and the weightings are shown below.

	Test %		Weighting		
	A	B	A	B	Combined %
Test 1	70%	36%	50%	50%	
Test 2	60%	40%	70%	30%	

Calculate the combined percentage (A plus B) for Test 1 and Test 2. Select your answers from the following four choices:

55%, 54%, 53%, 52%.

Answer 1

Answer 2

Question 16

The bar graph shows the percentage of pupils in a school who achieved GCSE grade C or above in five subjects, by sex.

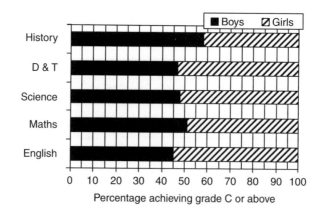

What proportion of the pupils who achieved grade C or above in English are boys? Give your answer as a fraction.

Answer

Mock test 2
(16 'on-screen' questions in 35 minutes)

Question 1
The table shows the percentages of a school's pupils achieving level 4 or above in teacher assessments, by sex, 2004–2006.

	Percentage of pupils at level 4+					
	Boys			Girls		
	2004	2005	2006	2004	2005	2006
English	72	74	76	84	84	84
Reading	79	82	80	87	87	87
Writing	55	56	60	71	72	75
Maths	73	75	77	74	75	75

Indicate all the true statements:

1   The percentage of pupils achieving level 4+ in each test from 2004 to 2006 was greater for girls than for boys.

Answer

2   Boys' performance in writing increased proportionately more than girls' performance in writing from 2004 to 2006.

Answer

3   If trends had continued, 78% of boys and 84% of girls would have achieved level 4+ in English in 2007.

Answer

Question 2
The table shows the number of pupils using different modes of transport to a school.

Car	Bus	Cycling	Walking	Other
	31	20	67	11

One pupil in every four travels to school by car. How many pupils travel to school by car?

Answer

Question 3

The pie chart shows the distribution of marks available in an English test.

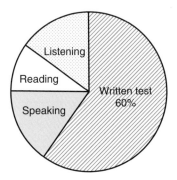

A pupil scored 75% in the written test and averaged 65% in the remaining tests. What was his overall percentage mark?

Answer [   ]

Question 4

A primary school calculates its pupil/teacher ratio (PTR) by dividing the number of pupils by the number of teachers. The number of teachers includes the Principal and any part-time staff. For part-time staff the full-time teaching equivalent is given by: part-time hours ÷ 25.

Calculate the PTR of a school with 170 pupils where the Principal has seven full-time teachers and one part-time teacher working 15 hours. Give your answer to one decimal place.

Answer [   ]

Question 5

A school compared Key Stage 2 points score with Key Stage 3 marks.

Choose the letter of the pupil that fits the description given.

1   This pupil scored 25 points at Key Stage 2 and the middle mark at Key Stage 3.

Answer [   ]

2   One-quarter of the pupils with 28 points at Key Stage 2 have Key Stage 3 marks above this pupil.

Answer [   ]

3   Three-quarters of the pupils with 26 points at Key Stage 2 have Key Stage 3 marks above this pupil.

Answer [   ]

Question 6
A pupil takes £100 on a school trip to Poland and exchanges £80 for Polish zlotys (zl) at an exchange rate £1.00 = 4.25 zl. He spends 250 zl in Poland and then exchanges the balance of his zlotys back into pounds at a rate of 4.50 zl = £1.00. How much money does he have on returning home?

Answer

Question 7
In a school's charity project, shoeboxes are covered in wrapping paper and filled with gifts. One shoebox is shown below.

13 cm

19 cm

32 cm

What is the minimum length of wrapping paper needed to cover all four sides of the box with a 2 cm overlap at the join? Give your answer in metres.

Answer [   ]

Question 8

A teacher set up a spreadsheet to calculate the cost of school trips, then entered the data for a farm trip.

	A	B	C	D
1	Items	Cost/item	Number	£ Total
2	Bus hire	176.00	1	176.00
3	Fee pupil	3.50	24	84.00
4	Fee adult	5.00	4	20.00
5				
6				
7		Total cost		280.00
8		Cost/person		10.00

Calculate the cost per person of the same farm trip with bus hire costing 6% more and fees costing 10% more.

Answer

Question 9

A pupil displayed his coursework data in a bar chart and a pie chart.

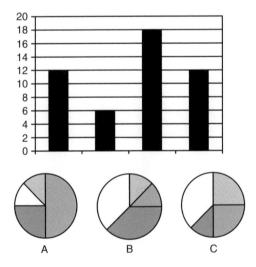

Which pie chart shows the same data as the bar chart?

Answer

Question 10

The table shows the distribution of pupils in a school according to year group.

Year	7	8	9	10	11	12	13	Total
Number	185	184	181	180			120	

How many pupils are on roll at the school if the mean number of pupils in years 7 to 11 is 181 and the ratio of pupils in year 11 to year 12 is 7:5?

Answer

Question 11

The graph shows the cumulative frequency of the hours spent on homework per week by a school's year 10 pupils.

Indicate all the true statements:

1 Most of the pupils spent up to 7 hours on homework.

Answer

2 About 90% of pupils spent at least 4 hours on homework.

Answer

3 The lower quartile is less than 6 hours.

Answer

Question 12

Six schools had the following proportion of pupils on free meals.

School	Proportion
A	10 out of 190
B	14%
C	1/9
D	0.06
E	1/20
F	17 out of 250

Which school had the highest proportion of pupils on free meals and which school had the lowest proportion on free meals?

Answer

Question 13

The scatter graph shows achievement at A-level plotted against prior achievement at GCSE.

Indicate all the true statements:

1   Two students achieved 120 points at A-level and less than 52 mean GCSE points.

Answer [   ]

2   Two-thirds of the students averaged less than 52 GCSE points.

Answer [   ]

3   All the students with mean GCSE points of 46 or more achieved at least 100 points at A-level.

Answer [   ]

Question 14

A school coach plans to leave Paris to arrive in Calais no later than 1230 hours. The coach averages 50 miles per hour and the distance from Paris to Calais is 300 kilometres. Use the approximation of 5 miles = 8 kilometres to find the latest time the coach can leave Paris.

Answer [   ]

Question 15

The table shows the GCSE grades achieved by Science pupils in classes 11a, 11b and 11c.

Grade	Number of pupils gaining each grade		
	Class 11a	Class 11b	Class 11c
A*	1	2	0
A	4	3	0
B	6	4	4
C	7	9	11
D	3	4	7
E	3	2	2
F	0	1	1
G	1	0	0
Total	25	25	25

Choose the letter (P, Q, R, S or T) in the next table that shows the correct A* to C results for the Science pupils shown above.

	Mean number of pupils gaining A* to G				
Mode	P	Q	R	S	T
A*	13	14	15	16	17
A	14	15	16	17	18
B	15	16	17	18	19
C	16	17	18	19	20
D	17	18	19	20	21
E	18	19	20	21	22
F	22	23	24	25	26
G	27	28	29	30	31

Answer

Question 16

The bar chart shows the number of pupils with and without special educational needs (SEN) in four schools, A, B, C and D.

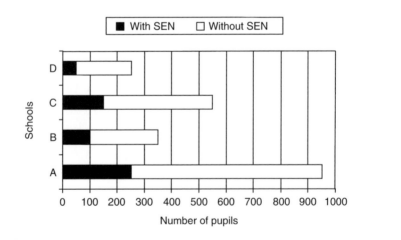

Which school had the highest proportion of pupils with special educational needs?

Answer

Part two

Literacy

Chapter 4
Spelling

Introduction

There are ten marks available for spelling. You will be tested on words that are part of everyday English as well as words found in a teacher's written vocabulary.

You might feel that spelling mistakes are not as impotant as content if the meaning remains clear. Spelling mistakes though serve as a focal point in a text and can distract the reader away from the message. Furthermore, if pupils, colleagues and parents spot a mistake it can create a negative impression of the writer. Spelling is either right or wrong and errors can dent your image as a professional.

Many students have trouble with spelling and rely on a computer's spell-checker function to expose misspellings and to suggest corrections. Although this may not diminish your spelling skills, you are more likely to repeat the errors instead of endeavouring to improve.

Rules of spelling

There are some simple rules that can help with spelling. If you know how to pronounce a word and are aware of the appropriate rule then it may be possible to work out how to spell a word rather than have to commit it to memory.

Mnemonics are short rhymes or verses that are intended to aid the spelling of words that are known to cause trouble, for example, when writing the word necessary, the correct number of <c's> and <s's> can be remembered from the mnemonic <one coffee with two sugars>. Unfortunately, many mnemonics are more difficult to remember than the spelling itself so these will not be considered further beyond the well-known rule <i before e except after c> and even this has its exceptions.

1 Problems with vowel sounds

Except for short words such as <my> and <by>, every word in the English language must contain one or more of the five vowels <a>, <e>, <i>, <o> and <u>; the remaining letters are consonants. Choosing between the vowel sounds <a>, <e> and <i> can prove troublesome. The following spellings are best learnt by heart.

admissible (<i> not <a>)
appearance (<a> not <e>)
cemetery (<e> not <a>)
definitely (<i> not <e> or <a>)
difference (<e> not <a>)
existence (<e> not <a>)
experience (<e> not <a>)
grammar (<a> not <e>)
grievance (<a> not <e>)
illegible (<i> not <a>)
irresistible (<i> not <a>)
maintenance (<a> not <e>)
occurrence (<e> not <a>)
permissible (<i> not <a>)
reference (<e> not <a>)
relevant (<a> not <e>)
respondent (<e> not <a>)

2 Problems with consonants

Spelling mistakes arise when the consonants <l>, <m>, <r>, <s> and <t> are unnecessarily doubled or when a double consonant is omitted. These mistakes arise because, unlike languages such as Welsh and Spanish, the single and double consonants are pronounced the same in English and the meaning is unchanged. The following words are commonly misspelt when the double consonant is omitted.

accommodate (not accomodate)
exaggerate (not exagerate)
excellent (not excelent)
generally (not generaly)

misspell (not mispell)
occurrence (not occurence)
referring (not refering)

In the following words a double consonant is frequently added where it is not needed.

disapprove (not dissapprove)
fulfil (not fulfill or fullfil)
harass (not harrass)
helpful (helpfully but not helpfull)
largely (not largelly)
until (not untill)

The following rules are helpful when adding suffixes, for example <-er>, <-est>, <-ing> and <-ed> to short words of one or two syllables. A syllable is the part of a word that has a single vowel sound, often with consonants, for example: be has one syllable, begin two syllables, and beginning three syllables.

i)   For one-syllable words, double the last consonant if the root word ends 'consonant-vowel-consonant' (CVC). Examples are shop and shopping; fit and fitted; big and biggest.

ii) For two-syllable words, double the last consonant if the spoken word is stressed on the last syllable rather than the first, as in begin and beginning; admit and admitting; or if the word ends in <l> as in travel and travelling; jewel and jeweller. The doubling rule only applies if the root word ends CVC, so for example, wide (VCV) and wider; clear (VVC) and clearest, fail (VVC) and failing, all use single consonants when adding a suffix.

Spelling test 1:
Double consonants (rules apply)

Choose either the single consonant spelling (A) or the double consonant spelling (B). Half the answers are As and half are Bs.

	Root	A	B
1	run	runing	running
2	bag	baged	bagged
3	hot	hoter	hotter
4	hard	harder	hardder
5	enrol	enroled	enrolled

	Root	A	B
6	excel	exceled	excelled
7	cancel	canceling	cancelling
8	defer	defered	deferred
9	enter	entered	enterred
10	ruin	ruining	ruinning
11	appear	appearing	appearring
12	diet	dieting	dietting
13	stoop	stooping	stoopping
14	wear	wearing	wearring
15	commit	commiting	committing
16	occur	occured	occurred
17	panel	paneling	panelling
18	happen	happened	happenned
19	open	opening	openning

The spellings in the following test fall outside the categories described earlier and are best learnt by heart. In some cases the wrong consonant has been doubled.

Spelling test 2:
Double consonants (learn by heart)

Choose the correct spelling (A) or (B). Half the answers are As and half are Bs.

	A	B
1	abreviate	abbreviate
2	acept	accept
3	agressive	aggressive
4	alowed	allowed
5	aproach	approach
6	cigarete	cigarette
7	elicit	ellicit

	A	**B**
8	family	familly
9	imediatley	immediately
10	inoculate	innoculate
11	mispelled	misspelled
12	mistakes	misstakes
13	normaly	normally
14	occasions	occassions
15	professional	proffessional
16	quarelling	quarrelling
17	recommend	reccommend
18	sincerely	sincerelly
19	tomorrow	tommorrow
20	vacuum	vaccuum

3 Problems with words ending in ‹ie›, ‹y› and ‹e›

i)   For words ending in <ie>, drop the <e> and change the <i> to a <y> when adding the suffix <-ing>; for example lie and lying, die and dying.

ii) For words ending in <y>, change the <y> to an <i> when adding the suffixes <ed>, <er> or <able> if the y is preceded by a consonant, but retain the <y> if it is preceded by a vowel or when adding the suffix <-ing>. For example, carry, carried, carrier and carriable, but enjoy, enjoyed, enjoyable and enjoying. When adding the suffix <ly>, change the <y> to an <i>; for example, necessary and necessarily, happy and happily (exceptions: shyly and coyly).

iii) For words ending in <e>, retain the <e> if the suffix begins with a consonant but drop it if it begins with a vowel. Examples: use and useful, but usable (no <e>); care and careful, but caring (no <e>); hope and hopeless, but hoping (no <e>). Exceptions to dropping the <e> occur when the root word ends in <-ee>, <-ce> and <-le>, for example: agree and agreeable, peace and peaceable, sale and saleable; exceptions to retaining the <e> include argue and argument, whole and wholly, true and truly.

4 Problems with <ie> and <ei> transposition

The mnemonic <i before e except after c> applies to most words where the vowel sound is <ee>. Examples are:

i)   before <e>: field, piece, tier, believe, hygiene, thief, yield, niece, siege;

ii)   except after <c>: receive, ceiling, conceive, perceive.

Exceptions to the rule are: seize, caffeine, either, forfeit, heinous, neither, weird, protein and species.

5 Problems with prefixes

i)   Add one <s> with <mis-> or <dis-> prefixes, as in heard and misheard, agree and disagree, appear and disappear; spell and misspell (add one s).

ii)   Add one <n> with <un-> or <in-> prefixes, as in usual and unusual, discreet and indiscreet; necessary and unnecessary (add one n).

6 Problems with homophones

These are pairs of words (and sometimes three words) that sound similar but are spelt differently and have different meanings (examples in brackets). The following list includes pairs of words that sound different but still give trouble.

Homophones and similar sounding words to learn by heart:

accept and except (receive something and exclude it)
adverse and averse (weather conditions and feelings against)
affect and having an effect (alter something and the result of it)
allot and a lot (to allocate and many)
aloud and allowed (out loud and permitted)
amoral and immoral (without morals and morally wrong)
ascent and assent (to 10,000 feet and agree to)
assure, insure and ensure (guarantee, against theft, the safety of)

baring and bearing (one's arm and bearing north west)
bated and baited (enthusiasm and a trap)
been and bean (there and baked bean)
born and borne (native born and costs borne by)
breach and breech (terms of an agreement and a birth)
broach and brooch (a topic and a jewellery item)

callus and callous (growth on skin and unfeeling)
check and cheque (the spelling of and pay money)
complacent and complaisant (after previous success and obliging)
compliment and complement (say nice things and go well together)
conscience and conscious (moral sense and awareness)
council and counsel (estate and guidance)
course and coarse (college and grit paper)
cue and queue (to action and in a line)
currant and current (bun and right now, also electric)

defuse and diffuse (a bomb and spreading out)
dependent and dependant (-child is a dependant (noun))
decent, dissent and descent (respectable, disagree and downhill)
discreet and discrete (tactful and separate from each other)
dough and doe (for bread and a female deer)
draft and draught (a letter and an excluder)
dual and duel (two of and a fight)

elicit and illicit (obtain and illegal)
guilt and gilt (ashamed and gold covered)
heel and heal (of shoe and cure)
into and in to (looked into the jar and looked in to see)
its and it's (belonging to it and a contraction of it is or it has)
licence and license (noun/verb; driving licence and to permit)
maybe and may be (perhaps and could be)
moral and morale (dilemma (good/bad); low (state of mind))
oral and aural (speaking test and listening test)

palate, palette and pallet (taste, paint and wooden)
passed and past (the test and the previous week)
personal and personnel (lives and colleagues)
piece and peace (portion and harmonious)
plain and plane (cooking and a vertical)
practice and practise (noun/verb; use practice tests to practise)
principal and principle (college head and of freedom of speech)
proceed and precede (to the checkout and lightning to thunder)
program and programme (computer and television)

raise and raze (a family and a building to the ground)
shoot and chute (a video and a playground slide)
scene and seen (scene of an accident and as seen on TV)
slight and sleight (small and crafty as in sleight of hand)

stair and stare (climb up and through the keyhole)
stationary and stationery (stopped and paper)
there, their and they're (look in (place); home (belonging); they are)
through and threw (a doorway and a ball)
to, too and two (we went to; too much or also; and 2)

waist and waste (measurement and rubbish)
wave and waive (your hand and your rights)
wait and weight (a long time and kilograms)
weather and whether (forecast and if)
whole and hole (all of it and in the ground)
write and right (a letter and correct)
your and you're (belonging to and a contraction of you are)

Spelling test 3:
100 words to spell correctly

	A	B	C	D
1	absence	absensce	abscence	abcense
2	accidently	accidentaly	accidantly	accidentally
3	accessable	accessible	accescible	acessibel
4	accomodate	accommodate	acommodate	accommadate
5	acheive	achieve	acheave	acheve
6	addresses	adressess	addreses	addresess
7	agresive	aggresive	agressive	aggressive
8	allwrite	allright	all right	alright
9	announcment	anouncement	announcement	anouncment
10	annonymous	anonymous	anonimous	annonimous
11	argument	arguement	argumeant	arguemeant
12	auxillary	auxilliary	auxillairy	auxiliary
13	appealling	appealing	apealing	apealling
14	begginning	begginning	begining	beginning
15	beleaved	beleived	believed	bellieved
16	believable	beleivable	beleavable	believible
17	benifitted	bennefitted	benefited	beneffited
18	britain	Britain	britan	Brittain
19	business	buisness	bisiness	businness
20	carefull	carful	carfull	careful
21	cemetery	cematery	cemetary	semetery

	A	B	C	D
22	chargable	chargeable	chargible	chargiable
23	colleages	colegues	colleuges	colleagues
24	comittee	commitee	committee	committy
25	conscientous	conscientious	consientous	concientous
26	contraversial	controversial	contravesal	controvesal
27	copys	copyies	copies	coppies
28	decesive	disisive	desesive	decisive
29	definitely	definetly	deffinitely	definately
30	detterrent	detterent	deterent	deterrent
31	diference	difference	differance	diferance
32	dissernible	discenrable	discennible	discernible
33	disappoint	dissappoint	disapoint	dissapoint
34	dissappear	disappear	dissapear	disapeare
35	disscretely	discretley	disscreetly	discreetly
36	endevour	endeavour	endeavor	endeavore
37	embarress	embarras	embarrass	emmbarras
38	existance	existence	existense	existanse
39	exstacy	exstasy	ecstacy	ecstasy
40	ennrolment	enrolement	enrollment	enrolment
41	fulfill	fullfill	fulfil	fullfil
42	forgetable	forgettable	forgetible	forgettible
43	gratefull	greatful	grateful	greatfull
44	greivence	grievance	grievence	greavence
45	harass	harrass	haras	harras
46	humouress	homourous	humoress	humorous
47	illegable	illegibel	ilegable	illegible
48	immediatley	immediatly	immediately	immedietly
49	innoculate	inoculate	inocculate	innocculate
50	irresistable	irrisistible	irresistible	iresistable
51	jepordy	jepardy	jeperdy	jeopardy
52	jewelery	jewellery	jewellry	jewellerey
53	laboratory	labratory	laborotory	laboratary
54	livleyhood	livelyhood	livlihood	livelihood
55	maintenance	maintainence	maintainence	maintenence
56	millenium	milenium	milennium	millennium
57	karioke	karaoke	karoake	karaoki
58	liase	liaize	liaise	leaise
59	manoeuvre	manouver	manouvre	manouever
60	michievoeus	mischevous	mischievous	mischeavous
61	neccessary	necessary	necesary	neccesary

	A	B	C	D
62	occasionally	occasionly	ocasionally	occasionaly
63	occurance	occurrence	occurence	occurrance
64	opulence	opulensce	opulescence	oppulence
65	parallel	parallell	parrallel	paralell
66	pavillion	parvillion	parvilion	pavilion
67	peddler	pedaler	peddlar	pedler
68	permisable	permissible	permisseable	pemissable
69	prescence	precence	presence	presense
70	precede	preceed	preeced	presede
71	proffession	proffesion	profession	profesion
72	privileged	priviledged	privilidged	priviliged
73	questionaire	questionnare	questionnaire	questionare
74	receit	reciept	reciet	receipt
75	recognise	recognize	reccognise	reccognize
76	recommend	reccomend	reccommend	recomend
77	recooperate	recuperate	recouperate	recuprate
78	rediculous	riddiculous	ridicullous	ridiculous
79	refferring	reffering	referring	refering
80	reference	refference	referrence	referance
81	rellevance	rellevence	relevance	rellevance
82	rythm	rythym	rhythym	rhythm
83	shedule	schedual	schedule	schedul
84	seperately	separately	sepperately	seperatly
85	successfull	succesful	successful	succesfull
86	supercede	superceed	supersede	superseed
87	susceptible	susceptable	susseptable	susseptible
88	temperary	temporary	temparary	temperery
89	tolerent	tollerent	tolerant	tollerant
90	tomorrow	tomorow	tommorow	tommorrow
91	umberella	umbrella	umberela	umberrela
92	unneccessary	unnecesary	unecessary	unnecessary
93	vaccum	vaccuum	vacuum	vacum
94	vanderlism	vandalism	vandelism	vandallism
95	vetnary	vetinary	vettinary	veterinary
96	wholly	wholey	wholley	wholy
97	xylofone	xylophone	zylophone	xylophon
98	yaught	yaucht	yauht	yacht
99	yoghurtt	yoghert	yoghurt	yoggurt
100	zellot	zealott	zealot	zeallot

Spelling test 4: Word selection

1 Disruptive behaviour may be .... by poor classroom management.

aggravated, agravated, agrivated, aggrivated

Answer [   ]

2 We have a green, yellow, and red card system for dealing with insolent, rude or .... behaviour.

beligerent, belligerent, belligerant, beligerant

Answer [   ]

3 Both student teachers and pupils have .... from lessons in citizenship.

benefitted, beniffited, benifitted, benefited

Answer [   ]

4 Our football team lost the match because we had become too .... and underestimated the opposition.

complaicent, complaisant, complacent, complaisent

Answer [   ]

5 Many schools are making a .... effort to offset their carbon-footprint.

consious, conscious, consciouse, concious

Answer [   ]

6 There has been much .... over school selection policies.

controversey, contraversy, controvercy, controversy

Answer [   ]

7 Higher education workers took part in a 'day of .... '.

descent, discent, dissent, disent

Answer [   ]

8 Classroom .... is essential for efficient teaching and learning.

disipline, dicipline, disciplin, discipline

Answer [   ]

9 My two Bs and a C were mildly ....

dissappointing, dissapointing, disappointing, disapointing

Answer [ ]

10 It would be .... to make a simple spelling mistake.

embarrassing, embarassing, embarrasing, embarasing

Answer [ ]

11 The debt crisis could .... teacher shortages.

ecsacerbate, exsacerbate, exaserbate, exacerbate

Answer [ ]

12 I sprained my ankle playing five-a-side football and it was .... painful.

extremely, extremelly, extreamly, extremley

Answer [ ]

13 The *x*-axis is used to plot the .... variable.

independent, independant, indipendent, indapendent

Answer [ ]

14 Unhealthy snack foods have become .... for some pupils.

irrisistible, irresistible, irrisistable, irresistable

Answer [ ]

15 There will be a meeting of the parents' .... committee on Friday week.

liason, liaison, liasion, liaision

Answer [ ]

16 Some university students may be eligible for a non-refundable .... grant.

maintainance, maintenence, maintenance, maintainence

Answer [ ]

17 A temporary post led to a .... position.

permenant, permanant, permanent, permenent

Answer [ ]

18   Her story stressed the virtues of hard work and ....

perseverence, perseverance, persaverance, persaverence

Answer

19   Our tutor spoke .... about his own problems with Maths.

poiniantly, poingnantly, poignantly, poynantly

Answer

20   Their sixth form college has a careers .... library where resources may be viewed but not borrowed.

reference, refrence, referance, refference

Answer

21   Should teachers dress more .... or at least appropriately?

professionaly, proffesionally, profesionally, professionally

Answer

22   It is .... that pupils with packed lunches are seated separately from those having hot dinners.

regrettable, regretable, reggretable, reggrettable

Answer

23   Prejudice and discrimination are part of .... education.

religous, religious, relligious, religouis

Answer

24   A letter starting Dear Mr or Mrs should end Yours ....

sincerly, sinserely, sincerely, sincerley

Answer

25   Old technology has been .... by interactive whiteboards.

superseded, superceded, superceeded, superseeded

Answer

26   The group booking was an .... good deal.

unbelievabley, unbelievably, unbelieveably, unbellievably

Answer

27   Children who behave .... at school may find themselves being sent home.

unacceptably, unacceptabley, unnacceptabley, unaceptably

Answer

28   Excessive testing can cause .... stress for pupils and teachers alike.

uneccesary, unneccessary, unnecesary, unnecessary

Answer

29   OFSTED stated .... that teaching was better in small schools with pro-portionately more good teachers.

unequivicolly, uniquivacally, unequivocally, uniquivacolly

Answer

30   The teacher proved that sound does not travel in a .... by pumping the air out of a bell-jar with the bell ringing.

vaccuum, vacuum, vaccum, vacume

Answer

Chapter 5

Punctuation

Introduction

There are fifteen marks available for punctuation, so a good result in this section goes a long way towards achieving the 29 marks needed for a pass. You will be given short passages of text that have had some of their punctuation marks removed, for example, commas, semi-colons, colons, apostrophes and full stops. To find the errors you need to look for natural breaks, lack of clear meaning, or inconsistencies in the punctuation. When you add punctuation, it must be consistent with the punctuation already in the passage.

The emphasis on correct punctuation reflects that careless mistakes or omissions can distort the meaning of text, as in:

<Today's school menu: Meat pie with mixed vegetables or baked beans, and potato wedges.>

which looks like one meal unless the menu meant:

<Today's school meal: Meat pie with mixed vegetables, or baked beans and potato wedges.>

A misplaced comma can introduce ambiguities in your written work and make it difficult to understand.

Problems with paragraphs

To help with reading and comprehension, a piece of prose (text) should be split into manageable chunks or paragraphs that deal with a distinct theme or aspect of the work. Each paragraph covers a single topic or expresses an argument within a few sentences. Every sentence in a paragraph should be relevant to its topic, with the first sentence (topic sentence) outlining the main thrust of the paragraph.

A new theme or topic begins with a new paragraph. If you have to subdivide text, it should be done on the basis of content rather than length; if the topic changes after only one sentence then you need a new paragraph. Long paragraphs (eg more than half a page) can be off-putting to readers so you can split a single topic into two or more paragraphs to make it more readable.

Problems with capital letters and full stops

A capital letter is used at the start of a sentence or any text. The pronoun <I> is always capitalized as is the first letter of a proper noun, for example <Mr Roberts>, <London> and <Private Peaceful>. Common nouns, for example <teacher>, <school> and <book> are only capitalized when they start a sentence or when they are linked to a title or an individual person's name:

> I wish to appeal against my son's failed application for a transfer to a new <secondary school>. Josh was baptized as an infant and attended a <catholic primary school>. I accept that he was never guaranteed a place at <St Peter's Catholic Secondary School>. However, I feel that his social and emotional development will improve at a <catholic school>. Josh's <headteacher>, Mr Collins, supported my application for Josh's transfer. It was <Headteacher> Collins who first said, 'He needs more pastoral support than we provide at this school.'

Problems with commas

A comma cannot be used to splice two sentences together. However, two mini-sentences (clauses) can be joined by a conjunction (connecting word) preceded by a comma. In the following example, two clauses have been joined with a comma instead of using the conjunctions <so> or <and>. Notice that the comma must be placed before the connecting word and not after it for the punctuation to be correct.

The girl enjoyed art, she looked forward to Art classes. ✗

The girl enjoyed art, so she looked forward to Art classes.

The girl enjoyed art, and she looked forward to Art classes.

A comma is not required with the conjunction <because>. One valuable tip when inserting a phrase into a clause is to remember that commas come in pairs, ie one before the phrase and one after it. The sentence will still read correctly if the phrase is taken out. Phrases and clauses are covered in the grammar section.

The girl enjoyed art, but she did not enjoy Art lessons.

The girl enjoyed ICT, and she looked forward to ICT classes.

The girl enjoyed music, yet she did not enjoy Music lessons.

The girl did not enjoy maths, nor did she enjoy Maths classes.

The girl looked forward to Art classes because she enjoyed art.

The pupils, who are not allowed into the classroom before the lesson begins, have to line up quietly in the corridor.

Commas are used to set off some opening words and phrases, such as <However,> <Therefore,> <Nevertheless,> <Meanwhile,> <In the first instance,> <On the other hand,> <All the same,>. They also are used to separate a string of items (three or more) in a sentence. There is no need to use a comma before the final and, except when it is necessary to clarify the meaning.

The teacher entered the classroom carrying a mixing palette, paints, brushes and a foam roller.

The teacher entered the classroom carrying a mixing palette, paints, brushes and a foam roller to wet the canvas. ✗

The teacher entered the classroom carrying a mixing palette, paints, brushes, and a foam roller to wet the canvas.

You may be unsure about whether a sentence needs a comma. The alternative would be to omit the comma and use a full stop followed by a new sentence. If you are in any doubt, then use a full stop and a new sentence. If the sentence is very short simply omit the comma.

Problems with semi-colons and colons

As a pause in a sentence, a semi-colon falls midway between a full stop and a comma. Unlike a comma, a semi-colon can be used to hold two linked sentences (clauses) together.

> The girl enjoyed art; she looked forward to art classes.

> The girl entered the room with glee; she enjoyed art classes and was looking forward to completing her final piece of coursework.

Semi-colons are also used to list information that has been introduced following a colon.

> The teacher entered the classroom carrying the following items: an easel and canvas; an assortment of paints, together with a tin of thinners; a palette to mix the paints on; a palette knife to mix the paints and to scrape the palette clean; four artists' brushes in incremental sizes.

Problems with the apostrophe and possession

The apostrophe is probably the most misused punctuation mark as it is often inserted where it is not needed. The most common error is to pluralize a noun with <'s> as in potato's. An apostrophe should only be used to show possession (ownership). If there is one owner (singular) then add <'s> to the end of the owner's name and if there is more than one owner (plural) add <'>. If a plural noun does not end in s then you need to add <'s>.

> There are five maths books left in the library.

> There are five maths book's left in the library. ✗

> The keen pupil's arrive early for the class. ✗

> The keen pupils arrive early for the class.

> I have the boy's books (the books belonging to one boy).

> I have the two boys' books (the books belonging to the two boys).

> It is the children's school.

> It is the childrens' school. ✗

Problems with contractions

When speaking we tend to contract two words to make a single, short version. These contractions use an apostrophe mark placed above the position of the missing letter or letters; the second word loses a letter or letters and the first word remains unchanged.

didn't and haven't instead of did not and have not (missing <o>);
he's instead of he is (missing <i>);
it's instead of it is (missing <i>) or it has (missing <ha>);
they'll instead of they will (missing <wi>);
might've instead of might have (missing <ha>); not might of.
who's instead of who is (this is different from whose, which is the possessive form of who, as in 'Whose is this book?').

Problems with speech marks and quotation marks

Speech marks ("----") are used to indicate the actual words spoken by someone (direct speech). A comma is placed inside the speech marks to separate the actual words spoken from the rest of the sentence. Alternatively, the sentence can be written in such a way that the comma comes before the speech marks and the direct speech starts with a capital letter.

"You took your time getting here," said Bond.

"Take a seat please James," Felix said.

Bond said, "You took your time coming."

Felix said, "Take a seat please James."

Any number of sentences can be included inside the direct speech without having to close the quotation marks and start new ones.

Evans frowned. "Sorry, I can't allow it. It's against the rules."

"Have you finished already?" said Evans. "Well done. I am pleased with your progress. You've earned more golden time."

"Hey, you there!" he yelled. "Come here. I can't wait all day."

Full stops, question marks and exclamation marks come before the closing speech marks and not after them.

> Joe frowned. "Sorry, I can't allow it."

> "Have you finished it?" said Joe. "Hey, you there!" he yelled.

Quotation marks ('---') are used to indicate a title; to quote a phrase from another source; and to highlight an unusual or questionable choice of word.

> 'Lord of the Flies' and 'Of Mice and Men' are GCSE favourites.

> My teacher asked me to think about the 'different types of prejudice' in the novel. To what extent is Lennie a victim of the prejudices of the 1930s 'depression era'?

Problems with question marks

A question mark takes the place of a full stop when a sentence asks a direct question; a question mark cannot take the place of a comma. Sentences that end with a question mark often begin How, Why, What, Where, When or Who. A question mark is not used with indirect (reported) questions but is part of direct speech.

> Was the numeracy test difficult?

> I asked, "Was the numeracy test difficult?"

> I asked if the numeracy test was difficult? ✗

Problems with brackets (parentheses)

Brackets are used to insert more information in a sentence without interrupting its flow; the sentence must read correctly after the words in brackets have been removed. The information in brackets often clarifies what has just been said or describes it in more detail.

> Gifted and talented students (those above the 90th percentile) must not lose their motivation between key stages.

> Our school's lessons cater for the more able pupils (the top 10%) who need to maintain their motivation between key stages.

Our school's lessons cater for the more able pupils (the top 10%) need to maintain their motivation between key stages. ✗

Punctuation test 1

Half the questions are punctuated correctly (✓) and half are not (✗)

1   Boys do better in Maths, girls in English and languages.

2   The Labour Government of 1964, and subsequent governments, supported the phasing out of grammar schools.

3   However there are still more than 150 grammar schools in England, and they remain popular with parents and young people.

4   To be certain of being seen, all pupils should wear clothing with yellow, orange, or light green fluorescent strips.

5   Semi-colons have several uses in punctuation, one of them is to hold two linked sentences together.

6   Pupil behaviour will improve by adopting the following

a consistent, whole school approach to classroom discipline;
an interactive style of teaching designed to increase motivation;
the inclusion of social skills training to improve self-awareness;
an incentive scheme that encourages positive behaviour.

7   A student's expectations of the course can be unrealistic.

8   Students' expectations of the course can be unrealistic.

9   Our school's rating was comparable with the average schools' rating for the Local Authority.

10   Parents expressed concerns about their children's safety, which meant that the school's annual trip had to be cancelled.

11   Most library's allow books to be renewed on-line.

12   Twelve books' can be taken out on your card at any one time.

13   If I had foreseen my low mark's I might have studied harder.

14   It's not easy working with mixed ability classes.

15   The school has achieved its LEA targets.

16   "I'm not surprised that foreign language teaching is in decline," said the head teacher. "Languages are no longer compulsory for 14 to 16 year olds, and there aren't enough jobs to go around."

Punctuation test 2

The following passage has twelve pieces of punctuation missing. Insert the missing punctuation in the correct places.

Should calculators be banned from the classroom

Calculators were invented to increase the speed of basic arithmetic calculations they were not intended to replace mental agility with numbers. However if too much time is spent on basic calculations then maths becomes tedious and pupils have less time to develop more advanced mathematical skills.

Problems involving fractions can rarely be solved with a calculator, even though addition, subtraction multiplication and division remain as key elements. On the other hand problems involving trigonometry calculus and graphs are greatly assisted by calculators.

Pupils dependency on calculators can impair number skills that require rough checks, such as rounding, approximation and estimation. In these situations, calculators need only be used when precision and accuracy are essential. Calculators should be allowed into the classroom, but not at the expense of paper and pencil skills after all speed is not everything, and what happens in the real world when a calculator is not available.

Punctuation test 3

The following passage has 15 pieces of punctuation missing. Insert the missing punctuation in the correct places.

Working children

If youre under 13 then apart from a few exceptions you cannot do paid work. At age 14 you can be employed in a wide range of jobs but these must not harm your health and development or affect your attendance at school.

By law young people aged 14 to 16 can only do light work. It is illegal to work on a building site or with heavy machinery you must not drive vehicles (including tractors on farms and you cannot work in kitchens and chip shops or serve alcohol, cigarettes and medicines

It is illegal for 14 to 16 year olds to work for more than

two hours on any school day

one hour before school starts

twelve hours in any school week.

Chapter 6

Grammar

Introduction

There are between 8 and 12 marks available for this section. The questions are based on a passage of prose split into half-finished sentences, each with a choice of four possible endings (clauses or phrases), only one of which uses the correct grammar. If you read back through the completed passage it should:

1 be grammatically acceptable and conform to the conventions of standard English;

2 make sense as a whole, with appropriate links between sentences;

3 be grammatically consistent from sentence to sentence;

4 avoid any ambiguity of meaning or any lack of clarity.

Teachers need a full grasp of the rules of formal written English. In the test you will have to spot mistakes in relation to:

● inconsistent tense/wrong or incomplete verb forms;

● lack of agreement between subject and verb; noun and pronoun;

● particles unrelated to a noun; incorrect or missing adverbial forms;

● problems with comparatives and superlatives;

● wrong or missing prepositions (eg different from/to);

- errors from speech, linked to contractions and the apostrophe;

- failure to observe where one sentence should end and another sentence should start;

- faulty sentence constructions with fragments left out;

- lack of cohesion between sentences when grammatical links are missed.

Review of grammar

Problems with verb forms and tense

Verbs are words that express action or a state of being, for example, to run, to speak, to work, to feel, to laugh, to be and to have. Regular present tense verbs can be changed into the simple past tense by adding the letters <ed> to the end. For example: walk becomes walked, and help becomes helped. Irregular verbs follow no such pattern. There are over two hundred irregular verbs. Some examples are:

awake/awoke; become/became; begin/began; break/broke; build/built; buy/bought; choose/chose; do/did; draw/drew; eat/ate; forget/forgot; freeze/froze; give/gave; get/got; go/went; have/had; hear/heard; hold/held; know/knew; leave/left; make/made; meet/met; read/read; ride/rode; send/sent; sing/sang; sink/sank; sit/sat; shake/shook; spell/spelt/spelled; swear/swore; swim/swam; take/took; wake/woke; wet/wet/wetted; write/wrote.

The verb <to be> takes the following forms in the present tense:

I am (first person singular; yourself)
you are (second person singular or plural; someone else)
we are (first person plural)
he is, she is, it is, Jack is (third person singular)
they are, Jack and Lucy are (third person plural)

All verbs must have a subject, eg Jack and Lucy (the subject) <are>. Plural verbs (unlike plural nouns) are not made by adding an <s> to the end; the <s> is sometimes removed to make a singular verb plural, for example <he walks> and they <walk>. The verb <to be> takes the singular form <was> in the past tense and the plural form <were> in the past tense. The verb <to have> takes the form <had> in the past tense.

I am late. You are late. He is late

Jack and Lucy are early

He walks, she walks and it walks

I walk, we walk, they walk and you walk

I was, he was, she was, it was

You were, they were, we were

I had, he had, she had, it had, you had, they had and we had

Future tense is expressed using the auxiliary verb <will> followed by another verb as in: I <will be> late for school. Sometimes <will> becomes separated from the other verb in the sentence as in: What time <will> you <leave> school? <Will> can also be combined with two other verbs to complete the sentence verb as in: English lessons <will be presented> in the library tomorrow. <Would> is used instead of <will> to express the future from some time in the past: I think class <will> finish early today (relates to now); I thought class <would> finish early yesterday (relates to earlier).

Past, present and future tenses with <to be> and <to have> are shown in the following table.

Tense	To be	To have
Present	I am, you are	I have, you have
	He is, she is, it is	He has, she has, it has
	We are, they are	We have, they have
	You are	You have
Past	I was, you were	I had, you had
	He was, she was, it was	He had, she had, it had
	We were, they were	We had, they had
	You were	You had
Future	I will be, you will be	I will have, you will have,
	we will be, they will be	we will have, they will have

Example: Jack has tried hard to improve his English skills this term but still needs to improve. He knows the rules of English grammar and how to construct a sentence but not:

a) what clear and precise expression are.

b) what clear and precise expression was.

c) what clear and precise expression were.

d) what clear and precise expression is.

All four choices are the same apart from the verb <to be> in the forms of <are> (plural present tense), <were> (plural past tense), <was> (singular past tense) and <is> (singular present tense). The correct answer is d).

> He knows the rules of English grammar and how to construct a sentence but not what clear and precise expression is.

Verb tenses must be consistent in a sentence, so <knows> in the example's question stem requires the present tense verb <is> in the answer text and not the past tense verbs <was> or <were>.

Verb–noun agreement is required, so the singular noun <expression> takes the singular verb <is> and not the plural verbs <are> or <were>.

The two adjectives <clear> and <precise> serve as distracters, tempting the reader into choosing <are>. You can remove these adjectives from the sentence to see the solution more clearly. Another trap finds a plural pronoun (eg they) used at the start of a sentence and attempts to link it with a plural verb at the end.

> He knows what <clear and precise> expression is.
> They know what <clear and precise> expression are. ✗
> They know what <clear and precise> expression is.
> They know what <clear and precise> expressions are.

Problems with participles

These are the <ing> form and the <ed> form of verbs. The <ing> form is the present participle and describes continuous action, as in: I am eating. It can be combined with all three tenses (past, present and future) to give the complete verb for the sentence, telling you what is, was or will be happening. For example: I am eating, was eating, will be eating. The <ed> form is the past participle and describes completed action. Participles can be combined with all three tenses to tell you what is, has or will be finished, as in: <I have helped>, <I had helped> and <I will have helped>. Past participles are often used with 'had' and many have irregular verbs.

Present tense	Past tense	Past participle (pp)
am	was	been
awake	awoke	awoken
blow	blew	blown
break	broke	broken
choose	chose	chosen
do	did	done

Present tense	Past tense	Past participle (pp)
drink	drank	drunk
draw	drew	drawn
eat	ate	eaten
fall	fell	fallen
freeze	froze	frozen
go	went	gone
have/has	had	had
give	gave	given
know	knew	known
lose	lost	lost
leave	left	left
ride	rode	ridden
ring	rang	rung
shake	shook	shaken
sing	sang	sung
swim	swam	swum
tear	tore	torn

Problems with nouns

These are the name of a person, place or thing and are often the subject of a sentence. Proper nouns are names of people, days of the week, titles of books etc, and are capitalized; some words can be both nouns and proper nouns as in: the British Government believes in small government. Collective nouns denote many individuals, for example, family, government, team, audience. Pronouns are used instead of nouns. They can have different forms depending on whether they form the subject or the object of the sentence as shown in the table below.

Subject	Object
I	me
you	you
he	him
she	her
we	us
they	them
it	it

A personal pronoun always uses the subjective case when it follows the verb 'to be' at the start of a sentence. In spoken English the subjective case sounds stilted so the objective case is often used. In written work the objective cases should only be used at the end of a sentence or with a preposition (in, at, on, with, between, after, before, from).

> It was I. It was he. It was they. (all subject)
> It was he (subject) and not her (object).
> It was I (subject) and not them (object).
> She and Jack (subject) can go with Lucy and me (object).
> We (subject) are quicker than them (object) but they (subject) are slower than us (object).
> Jack (subject) will leave before her and me (object).
> You and I (subject) will leave together.
> Between you and me; after them; before us; with me; from him.

Problems with adjectives: comparatives and superlatives

These modify nouns; they come in front of a noun and tell you more about it, for example: quick worker, clever pupil, careful teacher, two coins. An adjective that describes one noun or pronoun is known as a positive; comparatives compare two nouns and superlatives compare three or more nouns. For example <Lucy is tall> (positive), <Jack is taller> (comparative) and <James is the tallest (superlative) of all>. Usually we add <er> and <est> to make the two different comparisons, but there are exceptions. Examples are given in the following table.

Positive (1 noun)	Comparative (2 nouns)	Superlative (3 or more)
tall	taller	tallest
brave	braver	bravest
hard	harder	hardest
small	smaller	smallest
good	better	best
many/much	more	most
little	less	least
bad	worse	worst

Problems with adverbial forms

These words describe verbs. Adverbs are usually placed after the verb and many are made by adding <ly> to an adjective, for example quick and quickly, careful and carefully, easy and easily. Other adverbs include today, soon, now, before and immediately. Some 'doing' words can act as adjectives, verbs and adverbs as in <the careful nurse cared carefully for her patients>.

> She spoke loudly (adverb) in a loud (adjective) voice.
> I made a sudden (adjective) decision to leave suddenly (adverb).
> Josh is a happy (adjective) pupil and acts happily (adverb).

Problems with prepositions

These are usually placed before a noun or pronoun and show its relationship to something, for example <The exam is next year>. Some commonly used prepositions are: in, on, of, off, by, at, with, for, from, after, before, through, between, about, and around. Choosing between prepositions is sometimes difficult because there are no hard and fast rules so the correct preposition has to be memorized. The most difficult choice is often whether to use <to>, <with>, <for> or <from>, as in the following cases.

> It corresponds to (not with) the first chapter.
> I will correspond with (not to) the headmaster.
> We disagreed with the headmaster but agreed to differ.
> I have grown accustomed to it (not with it).
> The second edition was similar to (not with) the first edition.
> Results had improved compared with (not to) last year.
> We were disgusted with Jack and disgusted at his behaviour.

Problems with subject (noun) and verb agreement

The main subject noun and its verb should agree, ie either both are singular or both are plural. Collective nouns denoting many individuals are usually singular, whereas two singular subjects joined by <and> always take a plural verb.

> The pupil was ready to board the coach (he/she was ready).
> The team was ready for the kick-off (it was ready).
> The team were ready for the kick-off (it were ready) ✗
> Jack and the remaining pupil were leaving (they were leaving).
> The pupils were leaving (they were leaving).
> Jack and Lucy were leaving (they were leaving).
> Jack or Lucy was leaving (Jack was or Lucy was).
> Jack or Lucy were leaving (Jack were or Lucy were). ✗
> Jack, together with the other pupils, was leaving (he was leaving).

Confusion arises when the subject noun and the verb become separated.

> The results for the worst performing school is the most improved (the results is the most improved). ✗
> The results for the worst performing school are the most improved.

Problems with who and whom

Use <who> for the subject and <whom> for the object.

> I questioned the lecturer who I thought had made a mistake.
> I questioned the lecturer whom I thought had made a mistake. ✗
> I thought I had made a mistake so I questioned the lecturer whom I knew.
> I thought I had made a mistake so I questioned the lecturer who I knew. ✗

Problems with which and who

Use which (or that) with objects and who (or whom) with people.

> This classroom, which is larger, will accommodate the students.
> These are the students who need extra help.
> These are the students which need extra help. ✗

Problems with this, that, these and those

These is the plural of this and those is the plural of that.

> This is the new textbook. These are the new textbooks.
> That was the new edition. Those were the new editions.
> These is the new textbooks. ✗ That was the new editions. ✗

Grammar test 1

Half the sentences are correct (✓) and half are incorrect (✗)

1   Is the team ready?

2   We are happy if she is.

3   We was ill after he was.

4 It were faster than he was.

5 Either you are right or I am.

6 I were late and left alone.

7 It was you who was last.

8 The choir are singing.

9 The teacher was late and so misses his train.

10 It was extremely cold and the pipes had froze.

11 They shook hands and made up.

12 Carl speaks too loud in class.

13 Josh writes slowly and carefully.

14 Lucy and me are friends.

15 Emma can go with you and me.

16 It was they all along. (They did it; it was they all along. Note that 'It was them' is common in speech.)

17 Jack, Ben and Steve are tall, but Steve is the tallest.

18 Neither Moira nor Jane bring lunch.

19 Twenty per cent of the class are missing.

20 No pupils are ready.

21 Our team is ready so they will bat first.

22 Our pupils are ready so they will leave first.

23 The head teacher, along with the other teachers, are in class.

24 Homework compliance for the worst performing classes are the most improved.

25 The improvement in results for the schools with the highest proportion of pupils on free school meals was the greatest.

26 Every child, including those with special needs, have a fundamental right to education.

Sentence construction

The easiest sentences to understand are those that contain a single idea. When a sentence is crammed with too many ideas it becomes confusing and its thread is lost. If you introduce a second idea then make sure that it is properly linked with the main idea. Failure to link in the second idea leads to a run-on sentence that sounds disjointed. Sentence boundaries need to be observed, but a long sentence can be grammatically correct, if it is punctuated well and there are clear links between the ideas. If a sentence becomes too long or complex then it may be made clearer by splitting it in two; if you have any doubts then use a full stop to split it.

> The girl enjoyed art. She looked forward to Art classes.
> The girl enjoyed art she looked forward to Art classes. ✗
> The girl entered the room with glee because she enjoyed Art classes and looked forward to completing her coursework.
> The girl entered the room with glee. She enjoyed Art classes and looked forward to completing her coursework.

Problems with subject and object

In a sentence, the words are grouped together in a logical order that the person reading it can understand. Students with English as their first language will have no difficulty spotting faulty constructions, though it is worth recapping the basics.

All sentences must start with a capital letter and end with a full stop. They always contain a verb in the middle. A sentence begins with a subject, which is often a noun (person or place) and is often finished by adding an object; the object is the person or thing (a noun) at which the action (verb) is aimed. Not all sentences have an object, but they all have a subject. To give the sentence more meaning the last object is often joined to another noun to complete the picture. For example:

> The lecturer gave the students additional resources.
> (subject)   (verb)   (object)   (adjective)   (noun)

Problems with clauses and phrases

These are the main components of a sentence. A clause is a group of words that contain both a subject and an object. A main clause is a mini-sentence and most sentences contain one or more clauses. A phrase is a group of words that form part of a sentence but it does not contain both a subject and a verb, which are necessary for a sentence. If a phrase is removed from a sentence the remaining words still make sense (the clause is left). A subordinate clause contains both a subject and a verb but like a phrase it does not make sense without a main clause.

The bell rang (clause) and the pupils entered the room (clause).
The students, who are not allowed into the room (phrase), had to wait outside.
    (The students had to wait outside (main clause).)
The students had to wait outside (main clause) until the bell rang. (main clause with subordinate clause)
Until the bell rang. (subordinate clause on its own) ✗

If a phrase or a subordinate clause is added incorrectly to a main clause it can create grammatical ambiguities.

The school can hire the coach (main clause).
When it is ready, the school can hire the coach. ✗
(When the school is ready or when the coach is ready?)
The school can hire the coach when it is ready. ✗
(Probably 'when the coach is ready' but the ambiguity remains).

The meaning can be made clear by replacing the pronoun <it> with the appropriate noun:

The school can hire the coach when the coach is ready. OR
The school can hire the coach when the school is ready.

Alternatively, the word <to> can be added to either clause:

When the school is ready to, it can hire the coach. OR
When it is ready to, the school can hire the coach.

Problems with participles: related (✓) and unrelated (x)

A participle (eg <ing> or <ed> forms of the verb) in an opening phrase should relate to the noun in a clause that follows. If the noun becomes separated from the participle to which it relates then the meaning can become unclear.
    TIP: look for the answer that keeps the participle nearest to the noun.

Arriving late for school, the teacher saw the children. ✗
(Who arrived late, the teacher or the children?)
Arriving late for school, the children were seen by the teacher. ✓

In some cases it is better to recast the sentence:

The teacher saw the children arriving late for school.

Behaving inappropriately, the teacher asked the pupil to leave the class. ✗

(Whose behaviour was inappropriate, the teacher's or the pupil's?)
Behaving inappropriately, the pupil was asked by the teacher to leave the class. ✓
Alternatively, recast the sentence: The pupil, who was behaving inappropriately, was asked by the teacher to leave the class.

Increasingly expensive, some parents cannot afford school trips. ✗
Increasingly expensive, school trips are unaffordable for some parents. ✓
Alternatively, recast the sentence: School trips are becoming more expensive and some parents cannot afford them.

Grammar test 2

Half the sentences are constructed correctly (✓) and half are not (✗)

1   How many pupils are at grade C or above?

2   Are school dinners still unhealthy?

3   A well-balanced, healthy diet, low in saturated fat.

4   It's now or never.

5   Assessed by the popularity of A-level subjects last year, Maths and Science are making a comeback.

6   Seen as a candidate for A-star grades at A-level, the teacher thought she had every chance of a place at medical school.

7   Having acquired the skills of self-assessment and self-evaluation, teaching will benefit from reflective practitioners.

8   Recognizing the possibility of plagiarism, students must use the Harvard system of referencing for information taken off the internet.

9   Widely acknowledged as a seminal work on classroom management, the many facets of poor pupil behaviour were explored by Kounin (1970).

10 Shaken by the breach in confidentiality, changes were implemented by the head to prevent any more disclosures from taking place.

11   Between you and me.

12   That's all right then.

13   Between you and me, that's all right then.

14   Even though I had not expected to be on the winning team, it was disappointing for us to have lost the match.

15   Sarah went outside the library building to use the phone, to avoid disrupting other users.

16   Jackson states that the traditional method of teaching mathematics has failed pupils of low ability, believing that a whole-class interactive approach is the best way to reduce ability gaps.

Grammar test 3

Complete the following sentence by choosing the best of the four alternatives.

1   Our school trip to France ....
- a) because of the falling value of the Pound against the Euro will cost £15 more per pupil this year.
- b) because of the falling value of the Pound against the Euro will cost £15 more this year per pupil.
- c) will cost £15 per pupil more this year because of the falling value of the pound against the Euro.
- d) will cost £15 more per pupil this year because of the falling value of the pound against the Euro.

2   Judged by their evaluation forms, ...
- a) it was not found that larger classes were detrimental to the students' learning experiences.
- b) students did not find that larger class sizes were detrimental to their learning experiences.
- c) there was no detriment to students' learning experiences in larger classes
- d) larger classes were not found to be detrimental to the students' learning experiences.

3 GCSE results were very good again this year. The percentage that gained grades A* and A ....

    a) has risen to 35%

    b) will rise to 35%

    c) rose to 35%

    d) rising to 35%

Chapter 7

Comprehension

Introduction

There are between 8 and 12 marks available for the comprehension section. You will be given a passage of text to read and answer questions on. There are nine possible types of question (as outlined below); however, you will only be tested on a selection of these. Comprehension draws on the skills of reading and understanding. You need to elicit the facts (look for key words and phrases) rather than interpret what you think and feel. The nine question types require the ability to:

Choose the best main heading for the passage.
Choose the most appropriate sub-heading for paragraphs.
Check for inconsistencies between statements and text.
Choose statements that express correctly the meaning of text.
Match a statement with a given category.
Choose information from a list that relates to a question stem.
Summarize a paragraph in a sentence.
Present the key points of the passage.
Select the correct audience for text.

Comprehension passage 1

Read the following extract from a Department for Children, Schools and Families article, then answer the questions that follow.

Ministers said that schools needed to publicize financial support available for parents, and do everything they can to keep uniform and educational trip costs down.

A Cost of Schooling 2007 report looked at uniforms, PE kit, trips, lunch, travel, stationery, extra classes and voluntary contributions. The report found that the average total annual cost for primary schools was £684 and in secondary schools was £1195 – overall a rise of £34 or 4% since the previous report in 2003 (after adjustment for inflation). Eight in ten parents were happy with the costs of school – down from 90% in 2003, but almost four in ten found it very or quite difficult to meet the overall costs, up from 27% in 2003. Low-income families, especially those not working, found it most difficult.

Ministers said they were concerned that one in six parents had to buy all items of uniform and PE kit from a designated sole supplier or their school itself – despite clear government guidance that setting exclusive uniform deals with retailers disadvantages low income families. The mandatory Schools Admission Code places a statutory duty on all schools to ensure that admissions policies do not disadvantage any children. One-third of parents who buy clothes from sole suppliers were unhappy with the costs compared to just 9% who were free to buy clothes anywhere.

Ministers also said it was unacceptable and unlawful for any school to ask for compulsory contributions towards school trips which were part of the normal curriculum – as some schools admitted they do. Three quarters of all parents said they were asked to pay for the entire cost of a school trip – over nine out of ten paid the full cost of the residential trips and 68% for day trips. Only 38% knew that they should not pay for trips during school hours.

Task A: Choosing a main heading

You will be given a selection of possible headings and you must chose the one heading that best represents the entire passage of text, not just the introduction or one particular aspect or paragraph. Your choice of title should be informative and balanced rather than eye-catching or biased.

a) Cost of Schooling 2007 report.

b) School trips and uniforms too expensive for parents.

c) Ministers concerned over the cost of schooling.

d) Keeping the cost of schooling down for parents.

Task B: Choosing a sub-heading

Here you must choose the best sub-heading for a specified paragraph or two adjacent paragraphs. A sub-heading should cover the key points of the paragraph and flow naturally from the title of the piece.

Example: select the best sub-heading for the third paragraph.

a) Ministers concerned.

b) Low-income families disadvantaged.

c) Statutory duty placed on schools.

d) School uniforms and PE kit.

Task C: Comparing statements with the text

These questions check your understanding of the text using a series of statements that are either consistent or inconsistent with its meaning.

Example: read the following statements about the cost of schooling for parents and decide which are supported by the passage (✓), which are contradicted by it (✗) and which are neither upheld nor refuted by it (?).

The cost of schooling for parents.

a) Most parents are not unhappy with the costs of sole suppliers.

b) Trips that are not part of the school curriculum should be free.

c) Two in ten parents are unhappy with the costs of school.

d) Exclusive uniform deals disadvantage poorer families.

e) Almost 40% of parents have difficulties meeting school costs.

f) The school uniform should be affordable to all parents.

g) More parents found the overall costs difficult to meet in 2003.

h) Over 90% of parents paid the full cost of residential trips.

Task D: Choosing statements that express the meaning of text

Here you have to look back through the passage to find a key word or a phrase and then find the best match for it.

Example: which of the following statements is the closest meaning to: 'The mandatory Schools Admission Code (SAC) places a statutory duty on all schools' (paragraph 3)?

a) All schools should follow the SAC when admitting pupils.

b) Schools are legally obliged to admit disadvantaged pupils.

c) The SAC must not create economic hardship in families.

d) Admission policies must not deter families on low incomes.

e) Exclusive uniform deals appear inconsistent with the SAC.

Comprehension passage 2

Read the following extract from a Department for Children, Schools and Families press notice, and then answer the questions that follow.

The 'Teachers' Guarantee' goes alongside the Government's pupil and parent guarantees. The 'Pupil Guarantee' sets out what every young person should get during their school careers, including one-to-one or small group tuition for pupils falling behind at primary and the first year in secondary school. The 'Parent Guarantee' includes tougher Home–School Agreements, so every family understands their responsibilities and heads can take action against parents with the worst-behaved children if they do not comply and parents have their views listened to about how their child's school is doing.

The 'Teachers' Guarantee' includes new powers for teachers to tackle bad behaviour and dispels the myth that schools should have 'no contact policies'. The 'guarantee' also ensures that teachers get dedicated time to plan and prepare lessons and time to assess pupils' progress so teachers can continue to deliver high-quality lessons; support from the wider school workforce means that teachers are not tied up with photocopying and other administration tasks but in the classroom inspiring every child to learn.

The 'Pupil Guarantee' includes guaranteed one-on-one English and Maths tuition for primary pupils starting Key Stage 2 below expectations and unlikely to make two levels of progress by 11; statutory proper choice of high-quality learning routes at 14; guaranteed education or training at 16 and 17; specialist outside help for health and social problems; and a clear say on how their school is doing and how it can be improved.

The 'Parent Guarantee' includes: clearer information about their child's school performance; help and advice on choosing schools; high-quality advice about career and subject choices; closer involvement about their child's progress through access to a named personal tutor or teacher, with regular face-to-face and secure, online information about child's attainment, progress, Special Educational Needs, attendance and behaviour in secondary schools.

Behaviour expert and head teacher, Sir Alan Steer, has been monitoring progress on improving behaviour in schools since 2008 and concludes in his latest report that behaviour in schools is still good and continues to improve. His reports have provided invaluable insight into behaviour policies in schools which has led to stronger, clearer guidance for teachers on how they can make better use of their powers.

Task E: Matching categories with statements

In these questions you need to look back through the passage to find how a statement can be best categorized.

Example: look at the statements below and choose which refer to: Teachers' Guarantee [TG]; Pupil Guarantee [PuG]; Parent Guarantee [PaG]; School Policies [SP].

a) [   ] It provides information on jobs and subjects.

b) [   ] Heads can deal with badly behaved children's families.

c) [   ] It refers to the appraisal of pupils' progress.

d) [   ] It offers perspectives on pupil behaviour.

e) [   ] It uses personal tuition to close attainment gaps.

Task F: Choosing information from a list

You have to decide which phrases in a list contain accurate, relevant or implied information in relation to the question stem.

Example: select the four points that are the most appropriate to the Parent Guarantee.

a) It requires parents to comply with Home–School Agreements.

b) It reflects parents' views when decisions are made.

c) It provides access to a personal tutor or teacher.

d) It offers one-to-one or small-group tuition for pupils falling behind at primary school.

e) It provides more clarity on the performance of a child's school.

f) It empowers teachers to tackle bad behaviour.

g) It ensures that heads take action against parents' badly behaved children.

h) It provides information about pupil performance and school performance.

Task G: Summarizing paragraphs in a sentence

Here you have to choose a summary that reflects all the key points in one or more paragraphs.

Example: select the sentence that summarizes the information in the last paragraph most effectively.

a) School behaviour is still good and continues to improve, according to behaviour expert and head teacher, Sir Alan Steer.

b) Sir Alan Steer's reports on school behaviour have led to improvized guidance for teachers on using their powers.

c) A head teacher reports that behaviour in schools is improving and that teachers can make better use of their powers.

d) Teachers have clearer guidance on tackling bad behaviour thanks to progress reports by a head teacher and behaviour expert.

Comprehension passage 3

Read the following text from a Department for Children, Schools and Families news article, then answer the questions that follow.

The new non-statutory programme of learning for primary religious education (RE), will give local authorities and schools more ideas and support on how to develop their local RE curriculum. This will also make RE teaching consistent with the rest of the new primary curriculum.

The programme of learning covers the study of Christianity and the five principal religions – Buddhism, Islam, Judaism, Sikhism and Hinduism. It also recommends that pupils should be given the chance to learn about other religious traditions such as Baha'l faith, Jainism and Zoroastrianism, along with secular world views, like humanism, where appropriate.

Suggested topics for learning in primary RE lessons include: teaching about important festivals like Christmas, Easter, Pesach, Id-ul-Fitr or Diwali, and learning about different forms of religious expression, like music, dance and art; and thinking about responses to ethical questions.

The guidance to all schools was updated to take into account significant changes in types of schools and the curriculum, and to set out the Government's views on the importance of RE in the early 21st century. It reflects the multi-ethnic and multi-faith nature of our society and the Government's emphasis on community cohesion, which schools have a new duty to promote.

The guidance also includes a greater emphasis on personalizing learning to help pupils to better develop socially and emotionally as well as in their studies; information on how different types of schools should provide RE; more guidance on how to link RE to other subjects; and case studies on how teachers can work with local faith groups and use RE to support community cohesion.

Task H: Presenting the key points of the passage

Accuracy is important with these questions. Avoid choosing answers that appear likely but cannot be concluded from the evidence presented in the text.

Example: select the five statements that convey the most accurately what the 'programme of learning' involves.

a) Teaching about Christian and non-Christian festivals.

b) The importance of RE in community cohesion.

c) Links to other subjects such as citizenship.

d) Lessons on ethics.

e) How to engage with faith communities.

f) The RE topics that must be covered in the syllabus.

g) Guidance on RE provision for a range of schools.

h) A more individualized approach to learning.

Task I: Choosing the correct audience

Example: choose the most relevant audiences [M] and the least relevant audiences [L] for the text.

a) [   ] Primary schools

b) [   ] English teachers

c) [   ] School governors

d) [   ] Government

e) [   ] Local faith groups

f) [   ] RE teachers

Comprehension passage 4

Read the following text based on information from the teachernet site, and then answer the question that follows.

Safer School Partnerships (SSPs) aim to keep schools and pupils safe and reduce anti-social behaviour. The potential for setting up a partnership can be discussed with the local police, school heads, governors, local authority children's services and any group with an interest in young people's safety (eg Children's Trust).

Local schools and the police can be encouraged and supported to develop their existing links into formal SSP arrangements that set out the purpose, aim and the desired outcomes for the SSP. Public confidence and satisfaction measures will be a key driver in this process. All partners will need to agree a protocol setting out the working arrangement to ensure that each is clear about their role and responsibilities.

Once the chosen outcomes have been identified and agreed by the SSP, the partners' roles can be specified along with the steps to take, for example:

Chosen outcome: Reduce pupil and staff concern about 'trouble hotspots' on the school site, travel routes and in local area.
Partners' roles: Schools agree staffing, police agree to support; and both agree prevention and incident strategy.
Agreed action: Coordinated patrols at the beginning and end of the school day.

Effective monitoring and evaluation helps to compare actual outcomes of the SSP against original objectives. Evaluation should be ongoing. It should provide feedback to the partners and help the SSP to develop and expand. The evaluation can lead to new courses of action to meet desired outcomes, or can help identify good practice that can be rolled out more widely.

Task J: Placing the key points in the correct sequence

Select the four steps that best reflect the sequence of steps described in the passage.

1 Develop objectives

2 Gain public approval

3 Identify a need

4 Agree and implement the plan

5 Review impact and make improvements

6 Police agree support

7 Develop new outcomes

Choose four from seven

First step:

Second step:

Third step:

Fourth step:

Part three

Answers with explanations and Glossary

Answers

Chapter 1 Mental arithmetic

1 Warm-up exercise

1. two thousand five hundred and forty

2. four tens or 40

3. zero units

4. zero hundreds

5. 10000

6. 500000

7. 95432

8. 23459

9. fifty one million two hundred and forty thousand

10. 50 000 000 and fifty million

2 Warm-up exercise

1. 496

2. 213

3. 3147

4. 617

5. 429

6. 252

7. 214

8. 311

3 Warm-up exercise

1	63		6	450
2	96		7	95
3	132		8	99
4	120		9	300
5	92		10	1000

4 Warm-up exercise

1	806		5	425
2	2528		6	10000
3	1200		7	5511
4	5080		8	5082

5 Warm-up exercise

1	280		4	4900
2	6000		5	49000
3	490			

6 Warm-up exercise

1	4		5	410
2	62		6	59
3	113		7	244
4	53		8	125

7 Warm-up exercise

1	30		6	6
2	31		7	38
3	44		8	67
4	45		9	61
5	20		10	206

8 *Warm-up exercise*

1 14

2 13 (method: 10 + 3 = 13)

3 10

4 2 (method: 8 − 6 = 2)

5 14 (method: 10 + 4 = 14)

6 9

7 9

8 56

9 10

10 6

11 6

12 14 (method: 9 + 6 − 1 = 14)

9 *Warm-up exercise*

1 24

2 2

3 5

4 44

5 10 (method: 10 × 1 = 10)

6 21

7 39

8 57

9 3

10 36

11 5

12 9000

10 *Warm-up exercise*

1 1, 2, 3, 6

2 1, 2, 5, 10

3 1, 2, 4, 8, 16, 32

4 1, 2, 3, 5, 6, 9, 10, 15, 18, 30, 45, 90

5 1, 2, 4, 5, 10, 20, 25, 50, 100, 125, 250, 500

6 8 (method: factors of 24: 1, 2, 3, 4, 6, 8, 12, 24; factors of 32: for ease, look for the highest factors of 24 first and see if they fit 32: not 24, not 12; 8 × 4 = 32, so 8 is the highest common factor of 24 and 32)

7 15 (method: factors of 75: 1, 3, 5, 15, 25, 75; factors of 120; for ease look for the highest factors of 120 first and see if they are common to 75: not 120, not 60, not 30, not 20; 15 × 8 = 120, so 15 is the HCF of 75 and 120.)

8 4 (method: factors of 12: 1, 2, 3, 4, 6, 12; factors of 500; for ease look for the highest factors of 12 that will fit 500; not 12, not 6; 4 × 125 = 500, so 4 is the HCF of 12 and 500.)

11 Warm-up exercise

1	2×3	**5**	$3 \times 3 \times 3 \times 3$
2	$2 \times 3 \times 5$	**6**	$2 \times 2 \times 2 \times 3 \times 3 \times 3$
3	$3 \times 3 \times 7$	**7**	$5 \times 5 \times 5$
4	$2 \times 2 \times 3 \times 5 \times 7$	**8**	$7 \times 7 \times 7$

12 Warm-up exercise

1	2, 4, 6, 8	**4**	25, 50, 75, 100
2	12, 24, 36, 48	**5**	100, 200, 300, 400
3	20, 40, 60, 80		

Method for questions 6 to 10: look at the larger number and find the lowest multiple that the smaller number will divide into.

6   6 (method: 3 goes twice and 2 goes three times)

7   60 (method: 20 goes three times and 12 goes five times)

8   72 (method: 36 goes twice and 24 goes three times)

9   150 (method: 75 goes twice and 30 goes five times)

10   200 (method: 40 goes five times and 25 goes eight times)

13 Warm-up exercise

1	70	**6**	hundred
2	130	**7**	ten
3	100	**8**	hundred
4	140100	**9**	thousand
5	140000	**10**	ten thousand

14 *Warm-up exercise*

1	2022	**19**	54
2	610	**20**	80
3	195	**21**	26
4	2592	**22**	150
5	108	**23**	1, 2, 4, 5, 10, 20
6	64	**24**	2, 5
7	5625	**25**	1, 2, 3, 6, 7, 14, 21, 42
8	148473	**26**	2, 3, 7
9	10500	**27**	6, 12, 18, 24, 30, 36
10	250000	**28**	9, 18, 27, 36, 45, 54
11	11	**29**	18
12	39	**30**	100
13	224	**31**	250
14	72	**32**	60
15	130	**33**	ten
16	20	**34**	hundred
17	100	**35**	thousand
18	16		

15 *Warm-up exercise*

1	$\frac{1}{2}$	**6**	$\frac{3}{5}$
2	$\frac{3}{4}$	**7**	$\frac{1}{10}$
3	$\frac{1}{3}$	**8**	$\frac{19}{20}$
4	$\frac{5}{9}$	**9**	$\frac{2}{3}$
5	$\frac{2}{3}$	**10**	$\frac{2}{5}$

16 Warm-up exercise

1   $\dfrac{7}{8}$

2   $\dfrac{5}{6}$

3   $\dfrac{11}{10}$

4   $\dfrac{5}{4}$

5   1

6   $\dfrac{1}{2}$

7   $\dfrac{2}{3}$

8   $\dfrac{1}{5}$

17 Warm-up exercise

1   15

2   12

3   16

4   $\dfrac{7}{15}$

5   $\dfrac{11}{12}$

6   $\dfrac{3}{16}$

18 Warm-up exercise

1   $\dfrac{3}{4}$

2   $\dfrac{2}{3}$

3   $\dfrac{2}{5}$

4   $\dfrac{7}{8}$

5   $\dfrac{16}{50}$

6   $\dfrac{75}{1000}$

19 Warm-up exercise

1   $\dfrac{2}{27}$

2   $\dfrac{8}{45}$

3   $\dfrac{16}{63}$

4   $\dfrac{2}{27}$

5   $\dfrac{3}{500}$

6   $\dfrac{1}{2}$

7 $\dfrac{1}{3}$

8 $\dfrac{1}{4}$

9 $\dfrac{2}{27}$

10 $\dfrac{3}{10}$

20 Warm-up exercise

1 $\dfrac{2}{3}$

2 $\dfrac{3}{5}$

3 $\dfrac{3}{4}$

4 $\dfrac{1}{2}$

5 $\dfrac{5}{6}$

6 $\dfrac{2}{5}$

7 $\dfrac{1}{25}$

8 $\dfrac{1}{200}$

9 $\dfrac{3}{20}$

10 $\dfrac{2}{3}$

21 Warm-up exercise

1 $\dfrac{25}{12}$

2 $\dfrac{1}{6}$

3 $\dfrac{15}{8}$

4 $\dfrac{1}{2}$

5 $\dfrac{49}{10}$

6 $\dfrac{8}{3}$

7 $\dfrac{20}{9}$

8 $\dfrac{50}{1}$

22 Warm-up exercise

1 $\dfrac{7}{4}$

2 $\dfrac{11}{2}$

3 $\dfrac{17}{6}$

4 $\dfrac{27}{8}$

5 $\dfrac{67}{10}$ **8** $\dfrac{12}{5}$

6 $\dfrac{119}{100}$ **9** $\dfrac{7}{5}$

7 $\dfrac{6}{5}$

23 *Warm-up exercise*

1 $4\dfrac{1}{2}$ **4** $16\dfrac{2}{3}$

2 $5\dfrac{3}{4}$ **5** $5\dfrac{1}{4}$

3 $5\dfrac{1}{3}$ **6** $12\dfrac{1}{2}$

24 *Warm-up exercise*

1 $2\dfrac{1}{2}$ **5** $7\dfrac{1}{2}$

2 $4\dfrac{1}{2}$ **6** $\dfrac{3}{20}$

3 $3\dfrac{1}{2}$ **7** $\dfrac{1}{36}$

4 $10\dfrac{4}{5}$ **8** $\dfrac{1}{24}$

25 *Warm-up exercise*

1 $1\dfrac{2}{5}$ **4** 30

2 $4\dfrac{1}{4}$ **5** 64

3 8   **6** 72

7 $\dfrac{5}{8}$

8 $\dfrac{1}{4}$

9 $\dfrac{9}{20}$

10 $\dfrac{1}{2}$

11 $\dfrac{1}{4}$

12 $\dfrac{1}{12}$

13 2

14 $3\dfrac{3}{5}$

15 $\dfrac{1}{400}$

26 Warm-up exercise

1 3

2 14

3 8

4 8

5 8

6 5

7 3

8 1

9 5

27 Warm-up exercise

1 50p:10p

2 £12:£18

3 95:30

4 300:200:100

5 125:100:25

28 Warm-up exercise

1 $\dfrac{2}{20}; \dfrac{5}{20}; \dfrac{11}{20}; \dfrac{19}{20}$ (method: no calculation necessary: smallest numerator = smallest fraction when the denominators are the same)

2 $\dfrac{5}{125}; \dfrac{5}{25}; \dfrac{5}{20}; \dfrac{5}{10}$ (method: no calculations necessary: largest denominator = smallest fraction when the numerators are the same)

3 $\dfrac{2}{3}$ and $\dfrac{6}{9}$ (method: these are the only equivalent fractions)

4 $\dfrac{1}{5}; \dfrac{12}{40}; \dfrac{5}{10}; \dfrac{11}{20}$ (method: convert all to 40ths: 8/40; 12/40; 20/40; 22/40)

5 3 (method: find the equivalent fraction: $\frac{6}{10}$ cancels to $\frac{3}{5}$ by dividing the top and bottom by 2)

6 12 (method: find the equivalent fraction: $\frac{2}{3} = \frac{8}{12}$; noting that 8 is 4×2 and 12 is 4×3)

7 $\frac{1}{5}$

8 $\frac{3}{5}$

9 $\frac{1}{6}$

10 $\frac{7}{20}$

11 $\frac{5}{6}$

12 $\frac{3}{5}$

13 $\frac{1}{4}$

14 $\frac{2}{9}$

15 $\frac{1}{32}$ (method: change $\frac{1}{8}$ to $\frac{4}{32}$; then $\frac{5}{32} - \frac{4}{32} = \frac{1}{32}$)

16 $\frac{1}{12}$ (method: convert to twelfths then subtract: $\frac{9}{12} - \frac{8}{12} = \frac{1}{12}$)

17 $\frac{3}{8}$

18 $\frac{1}{6}$

19 $\frac{1}{20}$ (method: dividing by 6 is the same as multiplying by one-sixth, so re-write $\frac{3}{10} \div 6$ as $\frac{3}{10} \times \frac{1}{6}$ which is $\frac{3}{60}$ or $\frac{1}{20}$)

20 6

21 $\frac{1}{3}$

22 $3\frac{6}{7}$

23 $\frac{9}{2}$

24 3

25 $2\frac{1}{2}$

26 40

27 50

28 $6\frac{1}{8}$

29 $\frac{5}{7}$ (method: (easiest) change 4 wholes to sevenths $4 \times \frac{7}{7} = \frac{28}{7}$ then subtract from $\frac{33}{7}$ to leave $\frac{5}{7}$; (alternative): convert $\frac{33}{7}$ to a mixed number to give $4\frac{5}{7}$, then subtract 4 to leave $\frac{5}{7}$)

30 $\dfrac{5}{7}$ **32** 14

31 15:21   **33** i)   14
                                   ii)   18

29 Warm-up exercise

1 22.5   **4** 200.075

2 0.275   **5** 102.375

3 0.02

30 Warm-up exercise

	(a)	(b)	(c)	(d)
1	0.025	0.25	0.3	2.5
2	0.05	0.075	0.08	1.0
3	3.025	3.04	3.05	3.25
4	6.02	6.026	6.20	6.22
5	10.01	10.011	10.101	10.11

31 Warm-up exercise

1 1589.7   **5** 17170.3

2 769.2105   **6** 25

3 3172.9   **7** 5.8

4 0.0175   **8** 100

32 Warm-up exercise

1 8.96   **6** 160

2 20.02   **7** 3

3 0.3553   **8** 100.2

4 0.00544   **9** 2032

5 1.5015   **10** 14000

33 *Warm-up exercise*

1   1.7

2   12.45

3   8.03125

4   170 (method: 6.8 ÷ 0.04 becomes 680 ÷ 4 = 340 ÷ 2 = 170)

5   33.3 (method: 9.99 ÷ 0.3 becomes 99.9 ÷ 3 = 33.3)

6   11.1 (method: 5.55 ÷ 0.5 becomes 55.5 ÷ 5 = 11.1)

7   6 (method: 3.6 ÷ 0.6 becomes 36 ÷ 6 = 6)

8   60 (method: 9 ÷ 0.15 becomes 900 ÷ 15 = 300 ÷ 5 = 60)

9   1.2 (method: 1.44 ÷ 1.2 becomes 14.4 ÷ 12; we know that 12 × 12 is 144 from the times tables so 12 × 1.2 must be 14.4; answer 1.2)

10   62500 (method: 125 ÷ 0.002 becomes 125000 ÷ 2 = 62500)

11   20000 (method: 1000 ÷ 0.05 becomes 100000 ÷ 5 = 2000)

12   0.016

34 *Warm-up exercise*

1 $\dfrac{3}{5}$ (method: 0.6 = 6/10 = 3/5)

2 $\dfrac{3}{4}$ (method: 0.75 = 75/100; cancel by 25 to give = 3/4)

3 $\dfrac{5}{8}$ (method: 0.625 = 625/1000 = 125/200 = 25/40 = 5/8; cancelling by 5s)

4 $\dfrac{9}{10}$ (method: 0.9 = 9/10)

5 $\dfrac{1}{1000}$ (method: 0.001 = 1/1000)

6 $\dfrac{2}{25}$ (method: 0.08 = 8/100 = 4/50 = 2/25)

7 $\dfrac{19}{20}$ (method: 0.95 = 95/100 = 19/20)

8 $\dfrac{7}{4}$ (method: 1.75 = 175/100; cancel by 25 to give = 7/4)

9 $\dfrac{19}{8}$ (method: 2.375 = 2375/1000; cancel by 25; 2500 is 25 × 100; we have 2375 which is 125 less, or 5 × 25 less, so 2375 ÷ 25 = (100 − 5) = 95; 1000 ÷ 25 = 40; so we have 95/40 = 19/8; alternative method: keep cancelling by 5s until you reach 19/8)

35 Warm-up exercise

1   0.3 (method: 3/10 = 0.3)

2   0.25 (method: 1/4 = 0.25)

3   0.4 (method: 2/5 = 4/10 = 0.4; alternative method to dividing 2.0 by 5)

4   1.25 (method: 5/4 = 5.00 ÷ 4 = 1.25)

5   0.12 (method: 3/25 = 12/100 (multiplying top and bottom by 4) = 0.12; alternative method to dividing 3.00 by 25)

6   0.875 (method: 7/8 = 7.000 ÷ 8 = 0.875)

7   0.85 (method: 17/20 = 85/100 (multiplying top and bottom by 5) = 0.85; alternative method to dividing 17.00 by 20)

8   0.105 (method: 21/200 = 10.5/100 (dividing top and bottom by 2) = 0.105)

9   1.8 (method: 27/15 = 9/5 (cancelling by 3) = 18/10 (multiplying top and bottom by 2) = 1.8; alternative method to dividing 27.0 by 15 (or 9 by 5))

36 Warm-up exercise

1   a) (method: 12 × 5 = 60; nearest is a) 58.69)

2   b) (method: 24 ÷ 10 = 2.4; nearest is b) 2.51)

3   d) (method: 100 × half = 50, divided by 25 = 2; nearest is d) 1.95)

37 Warm-up exercise

1	1589.7	**5**	0.000175
2	3172.9	**6**	0.0000058
3	17170.3	**7**	33
4	769.2105	**8**	91

9   2400 (method: 120 ÷ 0.05 = 12000 ÷ 5 (multiply both numbers by 100 to remove the decimal point); 12000 ÷ 5 = 24000 ÷ 10 = 2400)

38 *Warm-up exercise*

1 $\frac{1}{5}$; 0.2

2 $\frac{1}{4}$; 0.25

3 $\frac{1}{10}$; 0.1

4 $\frac{3}{4}$; 0.75

5 $\frac{9}{10}$; 0.9

6 $\frac{9}{20}$; 0.45

7 $\frac{7}{20}$; 0.35

8 $\frac{11}{50}$; 0.22

9 $\frac{1}{50}$; 0.02

10 90; (50% = 50/100 = ½;
½ × 180 = 180/2 = 90)

11 60; (30% = 30/100 = 3/10;
3/10 × 200 = 600/10 = 60)

12 25; (10% = 10/100 = 1/10;
1/10 × 250 = 250/10 = 25)

13 12.5; (5% = 5/100 = 1/20;
1/20 × 250 = 250/20 = 12.5)

14 125; (62.5% = 62.5 ÷ 100
= 0.625; 0.625 x 200 = 125)

15 25; (2½% = 2.5% = 2.5 ÷ 100
= 0.025; 0.025 × 1000 = 25)

16 50%

17 1.5%

18 75%

19 105%

20 100%

21 0.5%

22 20%

23 36%

24 12.5%

25 85%

26 50%

27 40%

28 60%

29 25%

30 25920

39 *Warm-up exercise*

1 11 miles (method: 10 mins = 1/6 hr; 1/6 hr × 66 mph = 66 ÷ 6 = 11 miles)

2 1 mile (method: 5 mins = 1/12 hr; 1/12 hr × 12 mph = 1 mile)

3 10 miles (method: 15 mins = 1/4 hr; 1/4 hr × 40 mph = 10 miles)

4 2 miles (method: 40 mins = 40/60 hr = 2/3; 2/3 hr × 3 mph = 6/3 = 2 miles)

5   22.5 miles (method: 10 mph = 10 miles in 1 hr = 20 miles in 2 hrs; similarly: 10 miles in 1 hr = 2.5 miles in ¼ hr or 15 mins; adding these gives us 2 hrs + 15 mins = 20 miles + 2.5 miles = 22.5 miles)

6   10 km (method: 24 km/h = 24 km in 1 hr = 12 km in 30 mins; similarly 24 km in 1 hr = 2 km in 1/12 hr or 5 mins; subtracting these gives us 30 mins − 5 mins = 25 mins = 12 km − 2 km = 10 km)

7   13 miles (method: 780 miles in 1 hr = 780 ÷ 60 miles in 1 min = 78 ÷ 6 = 13 miles).

8   81 miles (method: 36 mph = 36 miles in 1 hr = 72 miles in 2 hrs, and 36/4 miles in ¼ hr = 9 miles in 15 mins; 72 + 9 = 81 miles)

40 *Warm-up exercise*

1   18.6 miles (method: 1 km = 0.62 miles; 30 km = 30 × 0.62 = 3 × 6.2 = 18.6 miles)

2   200 miles (method: 320 km × 5/8 = 40 × 5 = 200 miles)

3   225 miles (method: 360 km × 5/8 = 45 × 5 = 22.5 × 10 = 225 miles)

4   2.4 km (method: 5 miles = 8 km so 0.5 miles = 0.8 km then 1.5 miles = 3 × 0.8 = 2.4 km)

41 *Warm-up exercise*

1   28 mph (method: 84 miles in 3 hrs = 84/3 miles in 1 hr = 28 mph)

2   50 mph (method: 25 miles in 30 mins = 25 × 2 miles in 1 hr = 50 mph)

3   42 mph (method: 7 miles in 10 mins = 7 × 6 miles in 60 mins = 42 mph)

4   28 km/h (method: 21 km in 45 mins = 7 km in 15 mins (¼ hr) = 28 km/h)

5   60 km/h (method: 140 km in 2 hr 20 min = 140 km in (120 + 20) = 140 min = 1 km in 1 min = 60 km in 60 min = 60 km/h; alternative more mathematical method: 2 hr 20 min = 2 and 1/3 hr = 6/3 hr + 1/3 hr = 7/3 hr; to change 7/3 hr to 1 hr you multiply 7/3 by 3/7 (or simply invert the fraction); so distance travelled in 1 hr = 140 × 3/7 = 20 × 3 = 60 km/h)

6   18 mph (method: 12 miles in 40 mins = 3 miles in 10 min = 18 miles in 60 mins = 18 mph)

7   64 mph (method: 16 miles in 15 mins = 16 miles in 60 mins = 64 mph)

8 36 km/h (method: 27 km in 45 mins = 9 km in 15 mins = 36 km in 60 mins = 36 km/h)

9 72 km/h (method: 132 km in 1 hr and 50 mins = 132 km in 110 mins = 12 km in 10 mins = 72 km in 1 hr = 72 km/h)

42 Warm-up exercise

1 525 seconds (method: $8.75 \times 60 = 8 \times 60 + \frac{3}{4} \times 60 = 480 + 45 = 525$)

2 205 minutes (method: 3 hrs 25 mins = 180 mins + 25 mins = 205 mins)

3 7 (method: 168 hrs ÷ 24 hrs = 7 hrs)

4 0630 hrs (method: rewrite using the 24-hour clock 4-digit system)

5 2115 hrs (method: 9.15 + 12 hrs = 2115 hrs)

6 10:45 pm (method: 2245 − 12 hrs = 10.45 pm)

7 1810 hrs (method: 1445 + 3 hrs and 25 mins = 1445 + 4 hrs − 35 mins = 1845 − 35 mins = 1810 hrs)

8 1228 hrs (method: 1410 − 1 hr 42 mins = 1410 − 2 hr + 18 mins = 1228 hrs)

43 Easy questions

1 0920 hrs (method: 1200 hrs − (2 hrs 25 mins + 15 mins) = 1200 hrs − 2 hrs 40 mins = 1200 hrs − 3 hrs + 20 mins = 0920 hrs)

2 1040 hrs (method: 1225 hrs − 2 hrs + 15 mins = 1040 hrs)

3 7 days (method: 168 hrs divided by 24hrs/day = 7 days)

4 9 yrs 10 months (method: 11 yrs and 4 mnths − 18 mnths = 11 yrs and 4 mnths − 1 yr and 6 mnths = 11 yrs 4 mnths − 2 yr + 6 mnths = 9 yrs 10 mnths)

5 10 (method: 0850 hrs to 1530 hrs = 6 hrs 40 min (3 hrs 10 min to midday then 3 hrs 30 min after midday; subtract breaks of 1 hr 15 mins to leave 5 hrs and 25 mins, which is enough for 10 half-hour lessons)

6 1545 hrs (method: 10 × 30 mins + 90 mins = 5 hrs + 1 hr 30 min = 6 hrs 30 mins; 0915 hrs + 6 hrs 30 mins = 1545 hrs)

7 1315 (method: 50 + 50 + 10 = 110 mins = 1 hr 50 mins; 1505 − 1 hr 50 mins = 1315 hrs)

44 *Easy questions*

1   260 miles (method: 60 mph = 60 miles in 1 hr = 240 miles in 4 hrs and
     20 miles in 20 mins; total 240 + 20 = 260 miles)

2   312 miles (method: 72 mph = 72 miles in 1 hr = 288 miles in 4 hrs and
     24 miles in 20 mins = 312 miles)

3   90 miles (method: 40 mph = 40 miles in 1 hr = 80 miles in 2 hrs and
     10 miles in 15 mins; total 80 + 10 = 90 miles)

4   55 mph (method: 44 km in 30 mins = 88 km in 1 hr = 88 km/h. 88 ÷ 1.6 = 55)

5   48 km/h (method: divide both terms by 7 to get the distance travelled in
     5 minutes, then multiply by 12 to get the distance travelled in 1 hr (the speed);
     17.5 miles in 35 mins = 2.5 miles in 5 mins (dividing both terms by 7); then
     2.5 × 12 = 30 mph in 60 mins = multiply miles by 1.6 to get km/h = 48 km/h).

6   55 mph (method: 66 km in 45 mins = 22 km in 15 mins = 88 km/h;
     88 km/h = 88 ÷ 1.6 mph = 880 ÷ 16 = 110 ÷ 2 (dividing both terms by
     a factor of 8, or by 2 four times) = 55 mph)

7   1 hr 36 mins (method: use the SDT triangle: T = D/S so T = 6 miles
     (changed to kilometres) divided by 6 km/h = 6 × 1.6 ÷ 6 = 1.6 hrs
     = 1 hour + 0.6 × 60 mins = 36 mins; total 1 hour 36 mins)

8   1 hr 15 mins (method: T = D/S = 140 km (changed to miles)/70 mph
     = 140 ÷ 1.6 ÷ 70 = 2 ÷ 1.6 = 20/16 = 10/8 = 5/4 hrs = 1¼ hrs)

9   1250 hrs (method: 60 mph = 60 miles in 1 hr and 20 miles in 1/3 hr or 20 mins
     (note that 60 mph is 'a mile a minute'); total time = 1 hr 20 min add this to
     1130 hrs to give 1250 hrs)

45 *More difficult question*

1   a) 21 miles (method: 5 miles = 8 km; 8 km = 5 miles; 1 km = 5/8 miles;
         33.6 × 5/8 = 168/8 = 84/4 = 42/2 = 21 miles)
     b) 31.5 mph (method: average speed = total distance ÷ total time;
         total distance = 21 × 2 = 42 miles; total time = time C to L + time L to C;
         T = D/S, for CL = 21/36 = 7/12 hr = 7 × 5 mins = 35 mins; for
         LC = 21/28 = 3/4 hr = 45 mins; total time = 80 mins; average speed
         = 42 miles/80 mins = 21 miles in 40 mins = 10.5 miles in 20 mins; adding
         these last two give us = 31.5 miles in 60 mins or 31.5 mph)

Mental arithmetic test 1

1   In a school of three hundred and twenty-four pupils, one-sixth take free school meals. How many take free school meals?

$324 \div 6 = 300 \div 6 + 24 \div 6 = 50 + 4 = \mathbf{54}$

2   A school library contains one hundred and fifty-six books. If the number of non-fiction books is twice the number of fiction books, how many non-fiction books are there?

$2n + n = 156; \; 3n = 156; \; n = 52; \; 2n = \text{non-fiction} = \mathbf{104}$

3   If one gallon is equivalent to four point five litres, how many gallons are there in one litre? Give your answer as a fraction.

$1 \text{ gal} = 4.5 \text{ litre so } 1 \text{ litre} = 1 \div 4.5 \text{ gal} = 2 \div 9 = \mathbf{2/9 \text{ gal}}$

4   A school can buy ten books at nine pounds and ninety-five pence each or borrow the books from a library service at a cost of forty pounds. How much money will be saved by borrowing the books?

$9.95 \times 10 - 40 = 99.50 - 40 = \mathbf{£59.50}$

5   A school audio CD costs six pounds sixty pence plus VAT. If VAT is charged at twenty per cent, how much does the CD cost to the nearest penny?

$20\% = 20/100 = 1/5; \; £6.60/5 = £6/5 + 60p/5 = £1.20 + 12p = £1.32;$
$£6.60 + £1.32 = \mathbf{£7.92}$

6   Two hundred and forty pupils sat GCSE English. If forty-five per cent of the pupils achieved grade D or below, how many achieved grade C or above?

$100\% - 45\% = 55\%; \; 55\% \times 240 = 50\% \times 240 + 5\% \times 240$
$= 120 + 12 = \mathbf{132}$

7   A school bus arrives at the Tate Gallery at twelve hundred hours. The journey took two hours and twenty-five minutes excluding a fifteen-minute break. At what time did it set out?

Total time taken = 2 hr 25 min + 15 min = 2 hrs 40 min

1200 hr − 2hr 40 min = 1200 hr − 3hr + 20 min = **0920**

8   In a school run a pupil completed five miles around a four hundred metre track. How many laps of the track were completed if one mile is equivalent to one point six kilometres?

5 miles $= 5 \times 1.6 = 0.5 \times 16 = 8$ km

8 km $= 8 \times 1000$ m $= 8000$ m

$8000 \div 400 = 80 \div 4 = \mathbf{20 \text{ laps}}$

9 A ski trip to Switzerland costs seven hundred and fifty pounds and requires a twenty per cent deposit. What is the deposit in Swiss francs if one pound is equivalent to two Swiss francs?

£750 × 20% = 1/5 × £750 = £150 (or £750 × 0.2 = £75 × 2)

£150 × 2 Swiss francs per pound = **300 francs**

10 What is thirty-seven and one-half per cent as a fraction?

37.5% = 37.5/100 = 75/200 = 15/40 = **3/8**

11 A school playground measures twelve metres by thirteen point five metres. What is its area in metres squared?

12 × 13.5 = 12 × 10 + 12 × 3 + 12 × 0.5

= 120 + 36 + 6 = 156 + 6 = **162 m²**

12 An 11–18 comprehensive school has fifteen hundred and fifty pupils on roll, including three hundred and ten A-level students. What percentage of the pupils on roll are A-level students?

310 ÷ 1550 × 100% = 310 ÷ 155 × 10 = 2 × 10 = **20%**

Mental arithmetic test 2

1 School dinners cost one pound and eighty-five pence each. A pupil pays in advance for a week's dinners. What is the correct change in pence out of a ten pound note?

£1.85 × 5 = £2 × 5 – 15p × 5 = £10 – 75p; change = **75p**

2 A school with nine hundred and fifty places has an occupancy rate of ninety-four per cent. How many more pupils could it take?

6%: 0.06 × 950 = 6 × 9.5 = 6 × 10 – 6 × 0.5 = 60 – 3 = **57**

3 A school has two hundred and ninety boys and three hundred and ten girls. How many girls would you expect there to be in a representative sample of one hundred and twenty pupils?

290 + 310 = 600; 120 = 1/5 of 600

1/5 × 310 = 1/5 × 300 + 1/5 × 10 = 60 + 2 = **62**

4 An exam finished at twelve twenty-five hours having lasted one and three-quarter hours. At what time did the exam start?

1225 hrs – 1 hr 45 min = 1225 hrs – 2 hrs + 15 min = **1040**

5 In a sponsored run a pupil completed twenty laps around a four hundred metre track. How many miles did he complete if one kilometre equals five-eighths of a mile?

18 × 400 m = 7200 m = 7.2 km

7.2 km × 5/8 mile/km = **4.5 miles**

6 In a secondary school with nine hundred pupils, four out of every five pupils own a mobile phone. How many pupils do not own a mobile phone?

no phone = 1 out of 5 = 2 out of 10 = 20 out of 100

20 × 9 = **180** (avoids fractions, decimals, percentages)

7 A sponsored walk by five hundred pupils raised six thousand, nine hundred and fifty pounds for charity. What was the average amount raised per pupil?

6950 ÷ 500 = 6950 × 2 ÷ 1000

6950 × 2 = 7000 × 2 − 50 × 2 = 14000 − 100 = 13900 ÷ 1000 = **£13.90**

8 A school trip to the Tate Gallery took two hours and fifteen minutes by coach, travelling at an average speed of forty miles per hour. How far away was the gallery?

2 hours and 15 minutes = 2.25 hours

2.25 hours × 40 miles per hour = 22.5 × 4 = 88 + 2 = **90 miles**

9 A pupil gained thirty marks out of fifty in one Maths test and sixteen marks out of twenty-five in a second Maths test. What was the average percentage for the two tests assuming they were weighted equally?

30 out of 50 = 30 × 2 out of 100 = 60% (or 30/50 × 100%)

16 out of 25 = 16 × 4 out of 100 = 64% (or 16/25 × 100%)

average = **62%**

10 What is sixty-two and one-half per cent as a decimal fraction to one decimal place?

62.5% = 62.5 ÷ 100 = 0.625 = **0.63** (to 1 decimal points)

11 A school skiing trip costs seven hundred and twenty pounds per pupil with a fifteen per cent deposit. How much is the deposit in Euros if there are one point two five Euros to the pound?

15% × £720 = 0.15 × 720 = 15 × 7.2 = 72 + 36 = £108

£1 = €1.25; £108 = £108 × 1.25€/£ = €108 + €108 ÷ 4

= 108 + 27 = **€135**

12   Teachers at a school have four hours and twelve minutes contact time per day. What is the contact time per week?

4 hr × 5 + 12 min × 5 = 20 hr + 60 min = **21 hrs**

Mental arithmetic test 3

1   A pupil aged eleven years and four months has a reading age eighteen months below his actual age. What is his reading age?

subtract 18 months = subtract 2 years then add 6 months

= **9 years 10 months**

2   A geography school trip costs seventy pounds and the deposit is fourteen pounds. What percentage of the cost is the deposit?

14/70 × 100% = 14/7 × 10 = 2 × 10 = **20%**

3   Out of one hundred and forty-four pupils who sat GCSE English Literature, ninety achieved grades A to C. What fraction achieved grades A to C?

90/144 = 45/72 = 15/24 = **5/8**

4   In a primary school, five per cent of half-day sessions were missed through absence. If there were three hundred and eighty half-day sessions, how many were missed through absence?

10% × 380 = 38 half days so 5% = **19 half days**

5   How many school books at eight pounds and seventy-five pence each can be bought on a budget of one hundred pounds?

100 ÷ 8.75 = 400 ÷ (32 + 3) = 400 ÷ 35 = 10 + 1 = **11**

6   The highest mark in a Maths test was forty-six correct answers out of fifty questions and the lowest mark was twenty-five correct answers out of fifty questions. What is the difference between the highest and lowest marks in percentage points?

difference = 46 − 25 = 21 marks out of 50 = **42 percentage points**

7   A ski trip to Switzerland costs eight hundred pounds per pupil and requires a twenty-five per cent deposit. What is the deposit in Swiss francs if one hundred pounds buys two hundred and five Swiss francs?

£800 × 25% = 1/4 × £800 = £200

£200 × 205 francs per £100 = 205 × 2 = **410**

8 What is four-fifths as a percentage?

$1/5 \times 100\% = 100\% \div 5 = 20\%$, so

$4/5 \times 100\% = \mathbf{80\%}$

9 A fence is to be erected around a school playing field. The field is rectangular in shape and measures one hundred and twenty metres by ninety metres. What length of fence will be needed?

$120 \times 2 + 90 \times 2 = 240 + 180 = \mathbf{420\ m}$

10 What is two point five per cent as a fraction in its lowest terms?

$2.5\% = 2.5/100 = 5/200 = \mathbf{1/40}$

11 The teacher to pupil ratio on a school trip is not to be less than one to fifteen. If there are one hundred and seventy-two pupils going on the trip, how many teachers will be required?

$1:15 = 10:150 = 11:165 = 12:180 = \mathbf{12}$

12 A school day starts at eight-fifty am and finishes at three-thirty pm. Breaks total one hour and fifteen minutes. What is the maximum number of half-hour lessons possible per day?

0850 hrs add 10 min add 6 hr add 30 min to reach 1530 hrs
so lesson time = 6 hr 40 min − 1 hr 15 min breaks
= 5 hr 25 min = **10 lessons max**

Mental arithmetic test 4

1 At the start of a school day the library contains twelve thousand books. By the end of the day one hundred and twenty-three books have been loaned out and fifty-seven books have been returned. How many books are there in the library at the end of the day?

$12000 + 57 - 123 = 11900 + 157 - 123 = 11900 + 34 = \mathbf{11934}$

(borrow 100 from 12000 to add to 57)

2 In a class of twenty-five pupils, forty per cent are girls. How many boys are there in the class?

$100\% - 40\% = 60\%$; $0.6 \times 25 = 6 \times 2.5 = 12 + 3 = \mathbf{15}$

3 GCSE pupils take a Double Science or Single Science award. If Double Science is seven times more popular than the Single Science, what fraction of the pupils take Single Science?

7 double + 1 single = 8 parts; single = **1/8** (double = 7/8)

4 The cost of a school ski trip was six hundred and sixty pounds per pupil last year. This year the cost will increase by three per cent. What will be the cost per pupil this year? Give your answer to the nearest pound.

$660 \times 3\% = 660 \times 3 \div 100 = 6.60 \times 3 = £18 + £1.80 = £19.80$

$\text{Cost} = £660 + £19.80 = £679.80 = $ **£680**

5 What is zero point four five as a fraction?

$0.45 = 45 \div 100 = 45/100 = $ **9/20**

6 In a year group, seven out of every ten pupils achieved Key Stage 2. What percentage of the pupils failed to achieve Key Stage 2?

$7/10 \times 100\% = 70\%; 100\% - 70\% = $ **30%**

7 How many pieces of card measuring thirty centimetres by twenty centimetres can be cut from a sheet measuring one point five metres by one point one metres?

$1.5 \times 1.1 = 150 \times 110 \text{ cm} = 5 \text{ lengths} \times 5 \text{ widths} = $ **25 pieces**

8 A pupil is one point six metres tall. If there are two point five centimetres to the inch, how tall is the pupil in inches?

$1.6 \text{ metres} = 1.6 \times 100 \text{ cm} = 160 \text{ cm}$

$160 \div 2.5 = 1600 \div 25 = 6400 \div 100 = $ **64 inches**

9 School lessons start at a quarter past nine. There are ten lessons per day lasting thirty minutes each and breaks that total ninety minutes. What time does the school day finish?

$0915 + 5 \text{ hours lessons} + 1.5 \text{ hr breaks} = $ **1545 hrs**

10 A school minibus averages thirty miles per gallon. A teacher fills the tank with forty-five litres of fuel. How far can the minibus travel if one gallon is equivalent to four and one-half litres?

$45 \div 4.5 = 10; 10 \times 30 = $ **300 miles**

11 A test has a pass mark of seventy per cent. If there are thirty-five questions, what is the minimum number of correct answers necessary to pass the test?

$70\% \times 35 = 0.7 \times 35 = 7 \times 3.5 = 21 + 3.5 = 24.5 = $ **25**

12 In a school of one hundred and ninety-two pupils, seven-twelfths are boys. How many girls are there?

$192 \times 5/12 = 192 \div 12 \times 5 = (180 \div 12 + 12 \div 12) \times 5$

$(15 + 1) \times 5 = $ **80**

Mental arithmetic test 5

1   Four hundred and twenty-four pupils in a year group sit GCSE Maths. If seventy-nine pupils failed to achieve grade C or above, how many pupils did achieve grade C or above?

424 − 79 = 424 − 100 + 21 (subtract 100 then add back 21)

= 324 + 21 = **345**

2   The cost of a school trip to France was four hundred and thirty pounds last year. This year the trip will cost eleven per cent more. What will be the cost of the trip this year?

£430 + '11%' = 430 + '10%' + '1%'

= 430 + 43 + 4.3 = **£477.3**

(430 × 1.11 on a calculator)

3   GCSE pupils take Triple, Double or Single Science. If three-quarters take the Double Science and one-sixth take Single Science, how many take Triple Science?

1 (whole) − 3/4 − 1/6 LCD = 12 (twelfths)

12/12 − 9/12 − 2/12 = **1/12**

4   A school charges six pence per A4 page for photocopying, thirty pence for binding and twenty-five pence for a clear cover. What is the cost of two one-hundred page books bound with clear front and back covers?

1 book: 6p × 100 pages = £6 + 30p + 2 × 25p = £6.80

2 books = **£13.60**

5   What is twenty-two point five per cent as a decimal fraction?

22.5% = 22.5 ÷ 100 = **0.225**

6   The average weight of a class of eleven-year-old pupils is forty kilograms. What is this in pounds if one kilogram is equivalent to two point two pounds?

40 × 2.2 = 4 × 22 = **88 pounds**

7   A school teacher hires a minibus at fifty pounds per day plus the cost of the petrol used. The minibus uses one litre of fuel for every ten kilometres travelled. If fuel costs one pound and fifty pence per litre, how much would it cost for a one-day round trip of two hundred kilometres?

1 litre per 10 km = 20 litres per 200 km = 20 × £1.5 = 2 × £15

= £30; £30 + £50 = **£80**

8   The pass mark in a class test is sixty per cent. If there are forty-two questions, how many must be answered correctly to pass?

60% × 42 = 0.6 × 42 = 6 × 4.2 = 24 + 1.2 = 25.2 = **26**

9   What is zero point zero five multiplied by one thousand?

0.05 × 1000 = **50**

10   A school trip requires three forty-seater coaches to hold the pupils and teachers. Two of the coaches are full and the third is three-quarters full. How many teachers went on the trip if there was one teacher for every nine pupils?

40 + 40 + 30 = 110; 1 teacher + 9 pupils = 10 people;
teachers = 1/10 × 110 = **11 teachers** (and pupils = 99)

11   A school wildlife pond is four metres in diameter. What is the diameter of the pond on a fifty to one scale drawing?

4 m ÷ 50 = 400 cm ÷ 50 = 800 cm ÷ 100 = **8 cm**

12   A school day ends at five past three. There are two lessons in the afternoon each lasting fifty minutes with a ten-minute break in between. At what time does the first afternoon lesson begin?

50 min + 50 min + 10 min = 1 hr 50 min
1505 − 1 hr 50 min = 1505 − 2 hr + 10 min
= 1305 + 10 = **1315 hrs** (24 hour clock)

Chapter 2 General arithmetic

1 Warm-up exercise

1   2 (method: 6.08323 to 2 d.p.: 6.08$\underline{3}$23 = 6.08)

2   1 (method: 0.385426 to 5 d.p.: 0.38542$\underline{6}$ = 0.38543)

3   4 (method: 0.754 to 1 d.p. = 0.7$\underline{5}$4 = 0.8)

4   3 (method: 7.956 to 2 d.p. = 7.95$\underline{6}$ = 7.96)

2 Warm-up exercise

1   4.17 (method: 25 ÷ 6 = 4.166 = 4.17 to 2 d.p.)

2   14.2857 (method: 100 ÷ 7 = 14.28571 = 14.2857 to 4 d.p.)

3   10.4 (method: $3.45 \times 3 = 10.35 = 10.4$ to 1 d.p.)

4   44 (method: $14.5 \times 3 = 43.5 = 44$ to 0 d.p.)

5   81 (method: $325 \div 4 = 81.25 = 81$ to the nearest whole number)

6   160 (method: $1279 \div 8 = 159.8 = 160$ to the nearest whole number)

7   66 (method: $655 \div 10 = 65.5 = 66$ to the nearest whole number)

8   17 (method: $100 \div 6 = 16.6 = 17$ to the nearest whole number)

9   3 (method: $73 \div 22 = 3.3 = 3$ to the nearest whole number)

10   133 (method: $400 \div 3 = 133.3 = 133$ to the nearest whole number)

3 Warm-up exercise

1   3

2   5

3   30

4   17

5   115

4 Warm-up exercise

1   14

2   1

3   12

4   11.5 $((11+ 12) \div 2)$

5   8 $(15 - 7)$

5 Easy questions

1   4 (method: sum of numbers = average $\times$ number of numbers $= 6 \times 5 = 30$; then $30 = 3 + 10 + x + 5 + 8 = 26 + x$; so $x = 30 - 4$)

2   21 (method: sum of numbers = average $\times$ number of numbers $= 16 \times 8 = 128$; then $128 = 20 + y + 13 + 15 + 9 + 22 + 17 + 11$; group in pairs or threes to aid mental arithmetic: $128 = y + 33 + 24 + 50$; $128 = y + 107$; $y = 21$)

3 7 (method: sum of numbers = average × number of numbers = 8 × 9 = 72;
then 72 = 7 + 10 + 8 + x + 9 + 8 + 6 + 10 + 7; group to aid mental arithmetic:
72 = x + 25 + 17 + 16 + 7; 72 = x + 42 + 23 = 65; 72 = x + 65 = 7; so x = 7 and
the mode is 7 (three 7s))

4 5 (method: sum of numbers = average × number of numbers = 5 × 13 = 65; then
65 = 7 + 3 + 5 + 8 + 7 + x + 4 + 4 + 6 + 8 + 2 + 2 + 8; 65 = x + 64; x = 1
To find the median: 1, 2, 2, 3, 4, 4, 5̲, 6, 7, 7, 8, 8, 8)

5 2 (method: sum of scores = 1×5 + 2×1 + 3×3 + 4×1 + 5×0 = 5 + 2 + 9 + 4 + 0 = 20;
sum of frequencies (number of test takers) = 5 + 1 + 3 +1 + 0 = 10; finally we
have: mean = sum of (scores × frequency)/sum of frequencies = 20/10 = 2)

6 a) 1.3. Average = total number of brothers/sisters ÷ total number of pupils.
(0 × 7) + (1 × 8) + (2 × 6) + (3 × 3) + (4 × 1) = 8 + 12 + 9 + 4 = 33 brothers/
sisters; (to one decimal place) total number of pupils = 25; 33 ÷ 25 = 1.32
= 1.3 per pupil
   b) 1 (occurs most frequently: 8 out of 25 pupils)
   c) 1 (occurs at the 13th pupil ((25 + 1) ÷ 2) when ordered low to high; the 13th
pupil is within the box of 8 pupils: pupils 8th, 9th, 10th, 11th, 12th, 13th̲,
14th, 15th; the full 25 are 0,0,0,0,0,0,0,1,1,1,1,1,1̲,1,1,2,2,2,2,2,2,3,3,3,4)

Chapter 3 Statistics

1 Warm-up exercise

1 Food expenditure is the largest sector for girls

2 Appearance is the smallest sector for boys

3 Food expenditure is similar for boys and girls

4 One-quarter of the circle = 25%

5 Boys spend 1/2 × girls on appearance: 1/2 × 1/4 = 1/8

2 Warm-up exercise

1 20% are researchers

2 1/5 are researchers

3   35% = 35/100 = 7/20

4   16% = 16/100 = 8/50 = 4/25

5   0.35 + 0.16 = 0.51

6   0.2 × 160,000 = 2 × 16,000 = 32,000

7   16% + 20% − 35% = 1%; 1/100 × 160,000 = 1,600

8   0.09 × 160,000 = 9 × 1,600 = 10 × 1,600 − 1,600 = 14,400

9   Ratio of male to female = 5:1. Total parts = 5 + 1 = 6 parts and we have 1 part:
1/6 × 14,400 = 2,400

3 Warm-up exercise

1   Longest bar = Maths

2   Fifth longest = Design

3   History = 4%; 4 × 3 = 12% = English

4   Science double = 9%; 2/3 × 9% = 6% = French

5   10% = 1/10 = 0.1

6   12% + 13% = 25% = 1/4

7   10:12 = 5:6

8   180 × 5/6 = 30 × 5 = 150

9   12 + 10 + 6 + 8 + 4 + 9 + 13 = 62%

10   100% − 62% = 38% = 0.38

4 Easy questions

1   50% × 180 = 90

2   1/3 × 180 = 60; 60 × 70% = 60 × 0.7 = 6 × 7 = 42

3   60% × 180 − 50% × 180 = 10% × 180 = 18

4   54 pupils = 75% = 3/4; so 1/4 is 54 ÷ 3 = 18; 4/4 is 72

5 *Easy questions*

1   Level 4 (bar A is longer than bar B)

2   Bar B = 50 – 20 = 30; Bar A = 20 – 0 = 20; B:A = 30:20 = 3:2

6 *Easy questions*

1   140 miles in 3.5 hours = 280 ÷ 7 = 40 mph

2   2 hr – 1.5 hr = 30 minutes (stationary = no distance travelled = line horizontal)

3   0 hr = 1000 hr; 3.5 hr (1330) – 2 hr (midday) = 1.5 hr distance = 140 – 60 = 80 miles; 80 ÷ 1.5 = 53.3 = 53 mph

4   (3, 120)

7 *Easy questions*

1   Chemistry results show the least fluctuation

2   450 – 300 = 150

3   500 – 400 = 100

4   200; extend the line from 700 in 1990 to 200 by 2000 (or 100 fewer passes every two years = 500 fewer passes in 10 years)

8 *Easy questions*

1   70% read off the *y*-axis

2   Level 3–8 minus level 5–8 = 95% – 70% = 25%

3   75% = ¾

4   Level 3–8 minus level 5–8 = 95% – 75% = 20% = 1/5

9 *More difficult questions*

1   23 half-days = 11.5 days; 72% expected to achieve level 4+

2   Worse = coordinate point is below the line

3   Better = coordinate point is above the line

10 More difficult quesitons

1   Pupil E lies on a diagonal line that shows equal performance in both tests (equal *x* and *y* coordinates)

2   10 pupils below the diagonal line = better in writing

3   9 pupils above the diagonal line = better in arithmetic

4   12 pupils on or above the horizontal line

5   14 pupils to the right of the vertical line

6   11 pupils in the top right-hand corner

7   5 pupils in the bottom left-hand corner

8   Pupil F is the furthest away from the diagonal line with a difference of 10 marks

11 Warm-up exercise

1   St Moritz

2   July

3   Interlaken and Lake Geneva

4   September

5   Five

6   Four

7   All nine

8   10°C

9   Lake Lugano

10   September

11   23°C

12   6.1°C

13   10.6°C

14   Lake Lugano

15   Adelboden

16   11°C

12 *Easy questions*

1 $7 + 6 \times 2 + 5 \times 3 = 7 + 12 + 15 = 34$

2 $34 \div 6 = 5.67$ to 2 decimal places

13 *More difficult questions*

1   Points $= 6 \times 7 = 42 + 3 = 45$

2   Grade B (nearest to 45 points)

3   Grade D $(6 \times 5 + 3 = 30 + 3 = 33)$

4   Grade B $= 46$ points; $46 = 6 \times$ KS3 level $+ 3$, $46 (- 3) = 6$KS3; $43 = 6$KS3; KS3 $= 43 \div 6 = 7.17$, ie 7

5   Points $= 45 + 45 + 39 = 129$; $129 \div 3 = 43$

6 $42 \times 8 = 336 + 24 = 360$

7 $92 + 160 + 68 = 320$; $320 \div 8 = 40$

8 $5 \times 40 + 46 \times 2 = 292$; $314 - 292 = 22 =$ grade F

14 *More difficult questions*

1   Read down from C and across from C to find 4

2   Read across from C: $1 + 2 + 4 + 2 = 9$ (also see Total column)

3   Read down from A: $2 + 2 + 2 + 1 = 7$ (also see Total column)

4 $35 =$ total for French and total for Spanish (bottom corner)

5   Modal grade for French = most popular grade = grade C (occurs 9 times: $1 + 2 + 4 + 2 = 9$: see Total column; note that the answer is C not 9)

6   Grade C or above in Spanish $= C + B + A + A^* = 9 + 9 + 5 + 4 = 27$ pupils

7 $27 \div 35 \times 100\% = 77.1\%$

8   10 pupils lie to the left of the diagonal line drawn from A*A* to GG

15 *More difficult questions*

1   Total the bars: 150 students

2   Grade C or above = 133; 133 ÷ 150 × 100% = 88.7%

3   Modal = most popular = A grade

4   Median = (n + 1) ÷ 2 = 151 ÷ 2 = 75.5 (75th to 76th pupil) ie B grade (44th to 82nd pupil)

5   96% = 0.96; 0.96 × 150 = 144

16 *More difficult questions*

1   43 + 25 + 8 + 4 = 80; total = 125; 80 ÷ 125 × 100% = 64%

2   Ratio = 80:45 = 16:9

3   3 centre bars = 27 + 43 + 25 = 95; 95 ÷ 125 × 100 = 76%

17 *More difficult questions*

1   35

2   46

3   50

4   51 − 35 = 16

5   51 − 46 = 5

6   51 − 50 = 1

7   51 − 17 = 34

8   51 minus E and below = 46 (or read from the table)

9   34 ÷ 51 = 2 ÷ 3 = 2/3

10 46 ÷ 51 × 100 = 90.2%

11 Grade B and above = 51 minus grade C and below = 51 − 35 = 16; 16 ÷ 51 × 100 = 31.4%

18 *More difficult questions*

1   58

2   22

3   58 − 22 = 36

4   46

5   140

6   160 − 140 = 20

7   160 − 12 = 148

19 *More difficult questions*

1   18

2   20

3   13

4   30

5   100 − 30 = 70 (100 minus those with 16 marks and below); see the answer in 4: 30% achieved 16 or lower so 70% achieved more than 16

20 *More difficult questions*

1   Maths

2   English ('white line')

3   Science (shortest boxes)

4   Maths

5   Science (54% = median = half above and half below)

6   Science (similar length whiskers)

7   60% (upper quartile starts here)

8   Maths (the range of marks for the top 25% of pupils are shown by the length of the upper quartile whiskers)

9   80 × 50% = 40 (half of the marks are in the interquartile range)

10   English – all three subjects have their upper quartiles (whiskers) extending above 60% but only English has a proportion of the interquartile range above 60%

Answers to mock test 1

Question 1

$$((20 + 40) \times 1.8) - 40 = (60 \times 1.8) - 40 = (6 \times 18) - 40 = 108 - 40 = 68F$$

Question 2

1   True (end of whisker)

2   True (54 – 38 = 16)

3   False (one-quarter of the marks were 38 or below so three-quarters were above 38)

Question 3

1   False (36:32 = 9:8)

2   True (10:45 = 2:9)

3   False (30:50 = 3:5)

Question 4

1   False (the median mark occurs at 50% cumulative frequency)

2   True (the upper quartile occurs at 75% cumulative frequency with a mark of about 70%)

3   True (a mark of 50% has a cumulative frequency of less than 10% so at least 90% achieved a mark of 50% or more)

Question 5

1   True (100% – 89% = 11%)

2   False (we know the percentage but not the actual number)

3   True (A*–G minus A*–C = D, E, F, G = 100% – 92% = 8%; 8% = 8 per 100 = 2 per 25)

Question 6

£50. €13 = £10; £200 ÷ £10 = 20; 20 × €13 = €260. €260 − €195 = €65; €65 ÷ €13 = 5; 5 × £10 = £50

Question 7

1   False (A: 0.25 × 400 = 100; B: 0.3 × 330 = 99)

2   True (25% + 13% + 28% = 66%; 0.66 × 400 = 264)

3   True (30% + 9% + 33% = 72%; 25% + 13% + 28% = 66%)

Question 8

1   True (75 × 3 + 77 + 79) ÷ 5 = 381 ÷ 5 = 76.2

2   False (73.2 × 5 = 366 = total; 366 − 71 − 73 − 74 − 75 = 73%)

3   False (median: 86, 86, <u>86</u>, 87, 87)

Question 9

Arithmetic (36 ÷ 40 = 90%; 43 ÷ 50 = 86%; 54 ÷ 60 = 90%) ie Reading and Arithmetic have the highest scores. Smallest range: Arithmetic 29/60 = 48% (Reading 21/40 = 53%)

Question 10

12.6 kg (21 cm × 30 cm = 0.21 m × 0.3 m = 0.063 m^2; 0.063 m^2 × 80 g/m^2 = 5.04 g; 5.04 × 500 × 5 ÷ 1000 = 12.6 kg)

Question 11

1   True (for all five percentage intervals)

2   True (40+ interval displays the largest jump for 2000–2004)

3   False (in 2004, 90% of the pupils achieved KS2 level 4+ in schools where <10% of the pupils were entitled to free school meals)

Question 12

1   80% (8 out of 10 pupils)

2   2/3 (6 out of 9; check line by line)

3   60% (6 out of 10; check line by line)

Question 13

0815 (0845 − 30 = 0815; using the Swift ferry)

Question 14

2004 (school is slightly more than 10% above local authority)

Question 15

Test 1: 53% ($70 \times 0.5 + 36 \times 0.5 = 35 + 18 = 53$)

Test 2: 54% ($60 \times 0.7 + 40 \times 0.3 = 42 + 12 = 54$)

Question 16

9/20 (45% boys = 45/100 = 9/20)

Answers to mock test 2

Question 1

1   False (boys did better than girls in Maths in 2006)

2   True (boys: 55 to 60; 5/55 = 9%; girls 71 to 75; 4/71 = 5.6%)

3   True (2006 to 2007: boys +2%; girls +0%)

Question 2

43 (1 in 4; remainder = 3/4 = 129; 1/4 = 3/4 ÷ 3; 129 ÷ 3 = 43)

Question 3

71% (weighting: $75\% \times 0.6 + 65\% \times 0.4 = 45 + 26 = 71\%$)

Question 4

19.8 (PTR = 170 ÷ (1 + 7 + 15/25) = 170 ÷ (8 + 0.6) = 170 ÷ 8.6)

Question 5

1   Pupil E (is on the median line at 25 points)

2   Pupil P (is on the upper quartile at 28 points; ie 25% of pupils have higher marks and 75% have lower marks)

3   Pupil L (is on the lower quartile at 26 points)

Question 6

£40 (£80 × 4.25 zl/£ = 340 zl; 340 zl − 250 zl = 90 zl; 90 zl ÷ 4.50 zl/£ = £20; £20 + unconverted £20 = £40)

Question 7

0.64 (13 × 2 + 19 × 2 = 26 + 38 = 64 cm = 0.64 m)

Question 8

£10.75 (176 × 1.06 + (84 + 20) × 1.1) = £300.96; £300.96 ÷ 28 = £10.75

Question 9

C (two bars have the same height and two bars have different heights = A or C pie charts; longest bar to shortest bar = 3:1 = C)

Question 10

1150 (181 × 5 = 905; yr 11 = 905 − (185 + 184 + 181 + 180) = 175; yr 11: yr 12 = 7:5 = 175:125 (common factor of 25). Completing the table gives: total = 905 + 125 + 120 = 1150

Question 11

1   False (half not most; the median is at 7 hours)

2   True (10% CF is at 4 hours)

3   True (the lower quartile/25% CF is at about 5¾ hours)

Question 12

B highest; E lowest (convert each to a percentage: A = 5.3%; B = 14%; C = 11.1%; D = 6%; E = 5%; F = 6.8%)

Question 13

1   True (two students on the top line with <52 GCSE points)

2   True (14 out of 21 students have <52 GCSE points)

3   False (one student has 52 GCSE points)

Question 14

0845 (5 miles = 8 kilometres so 50 miles = 80 kilometres; 300 km ÷ 80 km/h = 30 ÷ 8 hr = 3 6/8 hours = 3 hours 45 min. Departs at 1230 – 3 hr 45 = 1230 – 4 hr + 15 min = 0845 hours)

Question 15

Letter Q (mean number of pupils A* to C grade for the three classes (see first table) = 18 (Class 11a) +18 (Class 11b) + 15 (Class 11c) = 51 divided by 3 = 17 pupils.

Then mode is C (first table): 7 + 9 + 11 = 27 = most frequent. Finally second table: mode 7 and mean 17 = letter Q).

Question 16

B (B = 0.4 or 40%; with to without ratios: A = 250:700 (0.36); B = 100:250 (0.4); C = 150:400 (0.375); D = 50:200 = 0.25)

Chapter 4 Spelling

Answers to spelling tests 1 and 2

	Test 1	Test 2
1	B	B
2	B	B
3	B	B
4	A	B
5	B	B
6	B	B
7	B	A
8	B	A
9	A	B
10	A	A
11	A	B
12	A	A
13	A	B
14	A	A
15	B	A
16	B	B
17	B	A
18	A	A
19	A	A
20	A	A

Answers to spelling test 3

1	A. absence	27	C. copies
2	D. accidentally	28	D. decisive
3	B. accessible	29	A. definitely
4	B. accommodate	30	D. deterrent
5	B. achieve	31	B. difference
6	A. addresses	32	D. discernible
7	D. aggressive	33	A. disappoint
8	C. all right	34	B. disappear
9	C. announcement	35	D. discreetly
10	B. anonymous	36	B. endeavour
11	A. argument	37	C. embarrass
12	D. auxiliary	38	B. existence
13	B. appealing	39	D. ecstasy
14	D. beginning	40	D. enrolment
15	C. believed	41	C. fulfil
16	A. believable	42	B. forgettable
17	C. benefited	43	C. grateful
18	B. Britain	44	B. grievance
19	A. business	45	A. harass
20	D. careful	46	D. humorous
21	A. cemetery	47	D. illegible
22	B. chargeable	48	C. immediately
23	D. colleagues	49	B. inoculate
24	C. committee	50	C. irresistible
25	B. conscientious	51	D. jeopardy
26	B. controversial	52	B. jewellery

53	A. laboratory	**77**	B. recuperate
54	D. livelihood	**78**	D. ridiculous
55	A. maintenance	**79**	C. referring
56	D. millennium	**80**	A. reference
57	B. karaoke	**81**	C. relevance
58	C. liaise	**82**	D. rhythm
59	A. manoeuvre	**83**	C. schedule
60	C. mischievous	**84**	B. separately
61	B. necessary	**85**	C. successful
62	A. occasionally	**86**	C. supersede
63	B. occurrence	**87**	A. susceptible
64	A. opulence	**88**	B. temporary
65	A. parallel	**89**	C. tolerant
66	D. pavilion	**90**	A. tomorrow
67	A. peddler	**91**	B. umbrella
68	B. permissible	**92**	D. unnecessary
69	C. presence	**93**	C. vacuum
70	A. precede	**94**	B. vandalism
71	C. profession	**95**	D. veterinary
72	A. privileged	**96**	A. wholly
73	C. questionnaire	**97**	B. xylophone
74	D. receipt	**98**	D. yacht
75	A. recognise and B. recognize are both correct	**99**	C. yoghurt
76	A. recommend	**100**	C. zealot

Answers to spelling test 4

1   Disruptive behaviour may be .... by poor classroom management.
aggravated, agravated, agrivated, aggrivated

2   We have a green, yellow and red card system for dealing with insolent, rude or .... behaviour.
beligerent, **belligerent**, belligerant, beligerant

3   Both student teachers and pupils have .... from lessons in citizenship.
benefitted, beniffited, benifitted, **benefited**

4   Our football team lost the match because we had become too .... and underestimated the opposition.
complaicent, complaisant, **complacent**, complaisent

5   Many schools are making a .... effort to offset their carbon-footprint.
consious, **conscious**, consciouse, concious

6   There has been much .... over school selection policies.
controversey, contraversy, controvercy, **controversy**

7   Higher education workers took part in a 'day of .... '.
descent, discent, **dissent**, disent

8   Classroom .... is essential for efficient teaching and learning.
disipline, dicipline, disciplin, **discipline**

9   My two B's and a C were mildly ....
dissappointing, dissapointing, **disappointing**, disapointing

10   It would be .... to make a simple spelling mistake.
embarrassing, embarassing, embarrasing, embarasing

11   The debt crisis could .... teacher shortages.
ecsacerbate, exsacerbate, exaserbate, **exacerbate**

12   I sprained my ankle playing five-a-side football and it was .... painful.
extremely, extremelly, extreamly, extremley

13   The *x*-axis is used to plot the .... variable.
independent, indepedant, indipident, indapendent

14   Unhealthy snack foods have become .... for some pupils.
irrisistibe, **irresistible**, irrisistable, irresistable

15   There will be a meeting of the parents' .... committee on Friday week.
liason, **liaison**, liasion, liaision

16   Some university students may be eligible for a non-refundable............ grant.
maintainance, maintenence, **maintenance**, maintainence

17   A temporary post led to a .... position.
permenant, permanant, **permanent**, permement

18   Her story stressed the virtues of hard work and ....
perseverence, **perseverance**, persaverance, persaverence

19   Our tutor spoke .... about his own problems with maths.
poiniantly, poingnantly, **poignantly**, poynantly

20   Their sixth form college has a career's .... library where resources may be viewed but not borrowed.
reference, refrence, referance, refference

21   Should teachers dress more .... or at least appropriately?
professionaly, proffesionally, profesionally, **professionally**

22   It is .... that pupils with packed lunches are seated separately from those having hot dinners.
regrettable, regretable, reggretable, reggrettable

23   Prejudice and discrimination are part of .... education.
religous, **religious**, relligious, religouis

24   A letter starting Dear Mr or Mrs should end Yours ....
sincerly, sinserely, **sincerely**, sincerley

25   Old technology has been .... by interactive whiteboards,
superseded, superceded, superceeded, superseeded

26   The group booking was an .... good deal.
unbelievabley, **unbelievably**, unbelieveably, unbellievably

27   Children who behave .... at school may find themselves being sent home.
unacceptably, unacceptabley, unnacceptabley, unaceptably

28   Excessive testing can cause .... stress for pupils and teachers alike.
uneccesary, unneccessary, unnecesary, **unnecessary**

29   OFSTED stated .... that teaching was better in small schools with pro-
portionately more good teachers.

unequivicolly, uniquivacally, **unequivocally**, uniquivacolly

30   The teacher proved that sound does not travel in a .... by pumping the
air out of a bell-jar with the bell ringing.

vaccuum, **vacuum**, vaccum, vacume

Chapter 5 Punctuation

Answers to punctuation test 1

1   Boys do better in Maths, girls in English and languages. ✗

(ie A run-on sentence. Boys do better in Maths. Girls do better in English
and languages. Boys do better in Maths, but girls do better in English and
languages.)

2   The Labour Government of 1964, and subsequent governments, supported the
phasing out of grammar schools. ✓

3   However there are still more than 150 grammar schools in England, and they
remain popular with parents and young people. ✗ (The comma is missing after
'However'.)

4   To be certain of being seen, all pupils should wear clothing with yellow, orange,
or light green fluorescent strips. ✗ (There is a comma missing; clearly all three
colours are meant to be fluorescent: To be certain of being seen, all pupils
should wear clothing with yellow, orange, or light green, fluorescent strips.)

5   Semi-colons have several uses in punctuation, one of them is to hold two linked
sentences together. ✗ (Semi-colons have several uses in punctuation; one of
them is to hold two linked sentences together.)

6   Pupil behaviour will improve by adopting the following ✗ (missing a colon after
the word 'following').

7   A student's expectations of the course can be unrealistic. ✓ (Singular noun with
possession.)

8   Students' expectations of the course can be unrealistic. ✓ (Plural noun ending
in s with possession.)

9   Our school's rating was comparable with the average schools' rating for the Local Authority. ✓ (Ordinary noun used in the singular case (one owner add 's) and in the plural case (more than one owner add '.)

10   Parents expressed concerns about their children's safety, which meant that the school's annual trip had to be cancelled. ✓ (Plural noun not ending in s and singular noun not ending in s.)

11   Most library's allow books to be renewed on-line. ✗ (ie Use the plural noun without an apostrophe (libraries).)

12   Twelve books' can be taken out on your card at any one time. ✗ (No apostrophe needed with an ordinary plural noun (books).)

13   If I had foreseen my low mark's I might have studied harder. ✗ (If I had foreseen my low marks I might have studied harder.)

14   It's not easy working with mixed ability classes. ✓ (It is.)

15   The school has achieved its LEA targets. ✓

16   "I'm not surprised that foreign language teaching is in decline," said the head teacher. "Languages are no longer compulsory for 14 to 16 year olds, and there aren't enough jobs to go around." ✓

Answers to punctuation test 2

Should calculators be banned from the classroom?(1)

Calculators were invented to increase the speed of basic arithmetic calculations. (2) They(3) were not intended to replace mental agility with numbers. However,(4) if too much time is spent on basic calculations then maths becomes tedious and pupils have less time to develop more advanced mathematical skills.

Problems involving fractions can rarely be solved with a calculator, even though addition, subtraction,(5) multiplication and division remain as key elements. On the other hand,(6) problems involving trigonometry,(7) calculus and graphs are greatly assisted by calculators.

Pupils'(8) dependency on calculators can impair number skills that require rough checks, such as rounding, approximation and estimation. In these situations, calculators need only be used when precision and accuracy are essential. Calculators should be allowed into the classroom, but not at the expense of paper and pencil skills.(9) After(10) all,(11) speed is not everything, and what happens in the real world when a calculator is not available?(12)

Answers to punctuation test 3

Working children

If you're(1) under 13,(2) then apart from a few exceptions,(3) you cannot do paid work. At age 14,(4) you can be employed in a wide range of jobs,(5) but these must not harm your health and development,(6) or affect your attendance at school.

By law,(7) young people aged 14 to 16 can only do light work. It is illegal to work on a building site or with heavy machinery.(8) You(9) must not drive vehicles (including tractors on farms)(10) and you cannot work in kitchens and chip shops,(11) or serve alcohol, cigarettes and medicines.(12)

It is illegal for 14 to 16 year olds to work for more than:(13)

two hours on any school day;(14)

one hour before school starts;(15)

twelve hours in any school week.

Chapter 6 Grammar

Answers to grammar test 1

1   Is the team ready? ✓

2   We are happy if she is. ✓

3   We (were) ill after he was. ✗

4   It (was) faster than he was. ✗

5   Either you are right or I am. ✓

6   I (was) late and left alone. ✗

7   It was you who was last. ✓

8   The choir (is) singing. ✗

9   The teacher was late and so (missed) his train. ✗

10   It was extremely cold and the pipes had (frozen). ✗

11   They shook hands and made up. ✓

12   Carl speaks too (loudly) in class. ✗

13   Josh writes slowly and carefully. ✓

14   Lucy and (I) are friends. ✗

15   Emma can go with you and me. ✓

16   It was they all along. ✓

17   Jack, Ben and Steve are tall, but Steve is the tallest. ✓

18   Neither Moira nor Jane bring lunch. ✓

19   Twenty per cent of the class (is) missing. ✗

20   No pupils are ready. ✓

21   Our team is ready so (it) will bat first. ✗

22   Our pupils are ready so they will leave first. ✓

23   The head teacher, along with the other teachers, (is) in class. ✗

24   Homework compliance for the worst performing classes (is) the most improved. ✗

25   The improvement in results for the schools with the highest proportion of pupils on free school meals was the greatest. ✓

26   Every child, including those with special needs, (has) a fundamental right to education. ✗

Answers to grammar test 2

1   How many pupils are at grade C or above? ✓

2   Are school dinners still unhealthy? ✓

3   A well-balanced, healthy diet, low in saturated fat. ✗ (missing verb)

4   It's now or never. ✓

5   Assessed by the popularity of A-level subjects last year, Maths and Science are making a comeback. ✓

6   Seen as a candidate for A-star grades at A-level, the teacher thought (the candidate) had every chance of a place at medical school. ✗

7   Teaching will benefit from reflective practitioners having acquired the skills of self-assessment and self-evaluation. ✗

8   Recognizing the possibility of plagiarism, students must use the Harvard system of referencing for information taken off the internet. ✓

9   Widely acknowledged as a seminal work on classroom management, Kounin (1970) explored the many facets of poor pupil behaviour. ✗

10   Shaken by the breach in confidentiality, the head implemented changes to pre-vent any more disclosures from taking place. ✗

11   Between you and me. ✗ (missing verb)

12   That's all right then. ✓

13   Between you and me, that's all right then. ✓

14   It was disappointing for us to have lost the match, even though I had not expected to be on the winning team. ✗

15   To avoid disrupting other users, Sarah went outside the library building to use the phone. ✗

16   Jackson states that the traditional method of teaching mathematics has failed pupils of low ability, believing that a whole-class interactive approach is the best way to reduce ability gaps. ✓

Answers to grammar test 3

1   d) Our school trip to France will cost £15 more per pupil this year because of the falling value of the pound against the Euro.

The main clause of the sentence is <Our school trip to France will cost £15 more per pupil this year>; this sentence is complete in itself making it the main clause. It should not be interrupted if the message is to remain clear. Answer a) is incorrect because the subordinate clause <because of the falling value of the Pound against the Euro> should come at the end. Answer b) is likewise incorrect, and a more logical order of words would be <£15 more per pupil this year>. Answer c) is incorrect because the meaning is ambiguous; it could mean either that the trip to France will cost £15 per pupil (eg more than the £10 charged last year) or it could mean that the trip will cost an extra £15 per pupil when compared with last year.

2   b) Judged by their evaluation forms, students did not find that larger class sizes were detrimental to their learning experiences.

The noun is at the beginning of the clause, as near as possible to the participle <Judged> and so avoids any ambiguity.

3   c) GCSE results were very good again this year. The percentage that gained grades A* and A rose to 35%.

The first sentence of the stem uses the past tense <were> as does the second sentence of the stem <gained>. For consistency, the answer should use the past tense <rose> of the irregular verb <rise>, not the present participle <rising>, or the past participle <risen>, or the future tense <will rise>.

Chapter 7 Comprehension

Task A: Choosing a main heading

a) Cost of Schooling 2007 report. ✗

b) School trips and uniforms too expensive for parents. ✗

c) Ministers concerned over the cost of schooling. ✗

d) Keeping the cost of schooling down for parents. ✓

Task B: Choosing a sub-heading

a) Ministers concerned. ✗

b) Low-income families disadvantaged. ✗

c) Statutory duty placed on schools. ✗

d) School uniforms and PE kit. ✓

Task C: Comparing statements with the text

a) Most parents are not unhappy with the costs of sole suppliers. ✓

b) Trips that are not part of the school curriculum should be free. ✗

c) Two in ten parents are unhappy with the costs of school. ?

d) Exclusive uniform deals disadvantage poorer families. ✓

e) Almost 40% of parents have difficulties meeting school costs. ✓

f) The school uniform should be affordable to all parents. ?

g) More parents found the overall costs difficult to meet in 2003. ✗

h) Over 90% of parents paid the full cost of residential trips. ✓

Explanation

a) ✓ Third paragraph, last sentence: One-third of parents who buy clothes from sole suppliers were unhappy with the costs; one-third is not most, so most are not unhappy is true.

b) ✗ Last paragraph, first sentence: Ministers also said it was unacceptable and unlawful for any school to ask for compulsory contributions towards school trips which were part of the normal curriculum. This is a direct contradiction of the statement.

c) **?** Second paragraph, third sentence: Eight in ten parents were happy with the costs of school; this does not categorically state that two in ten parents were unhappy.

d) ✓ Third paragraph, first sentence: Exclusive uniform deals with retailers disadvantage low income families.

e) ✓ Second paragraph, third sentence: Almost four in ten found it very or quite difficult to meet overall costs of schooling.

f) **?** Although this statement seems reasonable and is likely to be true, it cannot be related to any text in the passage.

g) ✗ Second paragraph, third sentence: four in ten found it very or quite difficult to meet overall costs of schooling, up from 27% in 2003. More parents found overall costs difficult to meet in 2003, should read 2007.

h) ✓ Last paragraph, second sentence: over nine out of ten paid the full cost of the residential trips.

Task D: Choosing statements that express the meaning of text

a) All schools should follow the SAC when admitting pupils. ✗

b) Schools are legally obliged to admit disadvantaged pupils. ✗

c) The SAC must not create economic hardship in families. ✗

d) Admission policies must not deter families on low incomes. ✓

e) Exclusive uniform deals appear inconsistent with the SAC. ✗

Task E: Matching categories with statements

a) [PaG] It provides information on jobs and subjects.

b) [PaG] Heads can deal with badly behaved children's families

c) [TG] It refers to the appraisal of pupils' progress.

d) [SP] It offers perspectives on pupil behaviour.

e) [PuG] It uses personal tuition to close attainment gaps.

Task F: Choosing information from a list

a) It requires parents to comply with Home–School Agreements. ✓

b) It reflects parents' views when decisions are made. ✗

c) It provides access to a personal tutor or teacher. ✓

d) It offers one-to-one or small-group tuition for pupils falling behind at primary school. ✗

e) It provides more clarity on the performance of a child's school. ✓

f) It empowers teachers to tackle bad behaviour. ✗

g) It ensures that heads take action against parents' badly behaved children. ✗

h) It provides information about pupil performance and school performance. ✓

Task G: Summarizing paragraphs in a sentence

a) School behaviour is still good and continues to improve, according to behaviour expert and head teacher, Sir Alan Steer. ✗

b) Sir Alan Steer's reports on school behaviour have led to improvized guidance for teachers on using their powers. ✗

c) A head teacher reports that behaviour in schools is improving and that teachers can make better use of their powers. ✓

d) Teachers have clearer guidance on tackling bad behaviour thanks to progress reports by a head teacher and behaviour expert. ✗

Task H: Presenting the key points of the passage

a) Teaching about Christian and non-Christian festivals. ✓

b) The importance of RE in community cohesion. ✓

c) Links to other subjects such as citizenship. ✗

d) Lessons on ethics. ✗

e) How to engage with faith communities. ✓

f) The RE topics that must be covered in the syllabus. ✗

g) Guidance on RE provision for a range of schools. ✓

h) A more individualized approach to learning. ✓

Task I: Choosing the correct audience

a) [M] Primary schools

b) [L] English teachers

c) [M] School governors

d) [L] Government

e) [M] Local faith groups

f) [M] RE teachers

Task J: Placing the key points in the correct sequence

First step: 3. Identify a need

Second step: 1. Develop objectives

Third step: 4. Agree and implement the plan

Fourth step: 5. Review impact and make improvements

Explanation:

Safer School Partnerships (SSPs) aim to keep schools and pupils safe and reduce anti-social behaviour. The potential for setting up a partnership can be discussed.

Local schools and the police can be encouraged and supported to develop their existing links into formal SSP arrangements that set out the purpose, aim and the desired outcomes for the SSP.

Once the chosen outcomes have been identified and agreed by the SSP, the partners' roles can be specified along with the steps to take.

The evaluation can lead to new courses of action to meet desired outcomes, or can help identify good practice that can be rolled out more widely.

Glossary

Numeracy

accuracy   Of a calculated value, the degree of closeness to the actual value. *See also* decimal place, rounding.

algebra   The use of letters and symbols in place of numbers to represent the structure of a formula or relationship between numbers, eg $y = mx + c$.

arithmetical operation   A function performed on two or more 'input' numbers to create a new number, for example addition, subtraction, multiplication or division. *See also* BIDMAS.

bar chart   A statistical graph where data is displayed as a series of vertical or horizontal bars; can be grouped or stacked.

BIDMAS   The order in which arithmetical operations should be performed. Brackets first, then indices ('powers'), followed by division and multiplication and finally addition and subtraction.

cohort   A statistical term used to define a population, eg this year's GCSE Maths cohort.

conversion   An exchange from one unit to another, eg pence to pounds, kilometres to metres, minutes to hours.

correlation   The strength of a relationship between two variables, such as grade in GCSE Maths versus QTS results.

cumulative frequency   The sum of the frequencies of an event recorded at different stages, from the beginning to the current position.

decimal fraction   A number less than 1, where a decimal point precedes the tenth, hundredth and thousandth, etc, eg 0.732.

decimal number   A number that contains both a whole number and a decimal fraction, eg 3.75.

decimal place (dp)   The number of digits to the right of a decimal point in a decimal number, eg 2.75 rounded to 1 dp = 2.8.

denominator   The bottom number of a fraction.

distribution   A statistical term that describes the spread of the data.

drag and drop questions   An on-screen test format. Here you click on the correct answer, then drag it to its correct location.

equation   A mathematical statement where two sides are shown to be equal to each other, eg $a = b + c$.

formula   Similar to an equation, but often identifies a rule, eg to convert centigrade to Fahrenheit, $F = 1.8C + 32$.

fraction   Part of a whole; the denominator (bottom number) is the number of equal parts that the numerator (top) is divided into.

frequency   A measure of the number of times that something occurs.

greater than symbol   The symbol >, eg x is greater than five: $x > 5$. *See also* less than symbol.

histogram   A statistical chart similar to a bar chart, but showing continuous data (such as age ranges) rather than discrete data (such as colours).

integer   A positive or negative whole number, or zero.

interquartile range   The difference between the upper quartile and the lower quartile, which represents the middle 50 per cent of the data.

KS   In education, Key Stages. KS1 = ages 4 to 7; KS2 = ages 7 to 11; KS3 = ages 11 to 14 and KS4 = ages 14 to 16.

less than symbol   The symbol <, eg x is less than five: $x < 5$. *See also* greater than symbol.

line graph   Data is plotted as a series of points joined by a line. Useful for showing trends, ie increases and decreases.

lower quartile   In statistics, the mark below which one-quarter of the marks lie (the bottom 25 per cent of the range); 75 per cent of the marks lie above it.

mean   A value found by dividing the total of all of a group of numbers by how many numbers there are in that group; the 'average'. *See also* median, mode.

measurement   The determination of length, weight, volume or any other quantity.

median   The middle number in a group of numbers that have been placed in numerical order, from smallest to the largest. *See also* mean, mode.

mental arithmetic   Maths calculations worked out without using a calculator.

mode   The value that occurs the most often in a group of numbers. *See also* mean, median.

more than symbol   *Same as* greater than symbol.

multiple choice questions   A test format. This offers several alternative answers where only one is correct, eg How many degrees make a full circle? a) 180 degrees b) 360 degrees c) 720 degrees.

NOR   Number on roll: the number of pupils enrolled at a school.

numerator   The top number of a fraction.

on-screen questions   A test format. The answers are inputted using the mouse or keyboard.

percentage   A fraction with a denominator of 100; a fraction expressed in hundredths.

percentage change   The change in a value (increase or decrease) divided by the original value and multiplied by 100 per cent.

percentage point   One per cent, used to express the difference between two percentages, eg the difference between 50 per cent and 60 per cent is 10 percentage points.

percentile   When results are placed in order of rank and divided into 100 equal parts, the value at or below which that percentage of results falls, eg the 70th percentile of test marks = the mark at or below which 70 per cent of results fall.

pie chart   A statistical graph in which a full circle (360 degrees) equals 100 per cent of the data. So half of the circle = 180 degrees = 50 per cent of the data; a quarter of the circle = 90 degrees = 25 per cent, etc.

prediction   The forecasting or extrapolation of pupils' future results based on current performance.

quartile   One of four quarter parts that results are divided into, by the 25th, 50th and 75th percentiles.

range   The difference between the highest value and the lowest value in a data spread.

ratio   Two or more quantities compared as either whole numbers or fractions, eg 2 parts to 5 parts; 2:5 = 2/7 and 5/7.

raw score   A result showing the actual marks that the person scored on a particular test. *See also* standardized score.

reading age   In a reading test, the national average score for a child. For example, most 10-year-olds will have a reading age of 10.

rounding   A method for simplifying numbers to the required level of accuracy, to the nearest 10, 100, 1000, etc, eg 178 rounded up to the nearest 10 = 180; to the nearest hundred = 200, etc.

SATs   Standardized Assessments Tasks; tests set at the end of each year to show pupil progress.

scale   1) A graduation mark on an axis or ruler. 2) A way of showing how one measurement relates to another, for example on a map or chart, eg 1:50,000 (1 cm on the map represents an actual distance of 50000 cm or 0.5 km).

scatter graph   A statistical graph plotting paired or related data, eg height and weight, to show whether or not a correlation exists.

sector   A 'wedge' or part of a circle, as used to represent a percentage in a pie chart. *See also* pie chart.

single response questions   A test format. Enter the correct answer in the way requested, eg if asked to 'express the amount to the nearest pound', for '£10.75' you would enter '£11'.

standardized score   A raw score that has been converted to take account of some other factor, eg age. *See also* raw score.

table   A way of displaying data using a grid.

tally chart   A table that is used to record the frequency of data.

trend   A pattern, sequence or series; the general direction in which something is tending to move, eg upwards or downwards.

two-way table   A table that is useful for comparing pupil performance in two subjects or in two different years.

unity   The number one (1).

Literacy

abbreviation   This is a shortened form of a word or words that are used to save time and space. Examples are: vs (versus), wrt (with reference to), asap (as soon as possible), eg (exempli gratia – for example), ie (id est – that is), pm (post meridian – in the afternoon).

acronym   An abbreviation made from the first letter of the words, for example TEFL (teaching English as a foreign language) and BTEC (Business and Technology Education Council).

adjectives   Words that describe (modify) nouns; for example, difficult subject, gifted pupil, conscientious teacher.

adverbs   Words that describe (modify) verbs; many end in -ly, for example walked quickly, spoke quietly, tested annually.

agreement (noun–verb)   Singular nouns take the singular verb and plural nouns take the plural verb; for example Jack improves daily, Jack and Phoebe improve daily.

analogous   These are words that have different meanings but are related in some way, eg car and van, house and castle.

antonyms   These are pairs of words that have opposite meanings, eg slow and fast, arrive and depart.

apostrophe (')   A punctuation that shows possession, as in Katie's shoe, and used in contractions to indicate a missing letter or letters, as in couldn't (could not) and we'll (we will).

articles   These are 'a', 'an' and 'the' as applied to a noun.

aural test   This is a test that requires listening and understanding.

brackets   *See* parentheses.

clause   A mini-sentence (contains a verb) that either stands on its own, or forms part of a complex sentence with other clauses. For example: She spoke (main clause) and the rest of the class listened (subordinate clause).

cohesion   Sentences should link together coherently. Lack of cohesion occurs when, for example, a pronoun fails to refer back to its noun, as in: Luke needed his pass for the school bus. It was a new one and had only just arrived.

colon (:)   This is punctuation that introduces a list, an explanation, or a definition.

comma (,)   This is punctuation that sets off opening words, adds phrases, or separates a list of items.

comma splice   Two sentences joined incorrectly with a comma.

comparatives   These are adjectives that compare two nouns, for example the better of the two teams.

comprehension   The ability to read, understand and evaluate a passage of text.

conjunctions   Co-ordinating conjunctions are the short joining words – but, and, or, so, for – that are used to join two words, clauses or phrases. A subordinating conjunction is a joining word between a main clause and a subordinating clause. Examples are: after, although, because, before, if, since, though, when, unless, and until.

consonants   All the letters of the English alphabet that are not vowels.

contractions   *See* apostrophe.

demonstratives   These are this/that, used with singular nouns, and these/those used with plural nouns. For example: this book here, these books here; that book over there, those books over there.

exclamation mark (!)   A punctuation mark placed at the end of a sentence to express strong feelings. For example: Stop that right now!

full stop (.)   A punctuation mark used to indicate the end of a sentence. It is often used with abbreviations but not with acronyms.

grammar   The rules of English language that govern sentence construction.

homophones (and homonyms)   These are words that sound similar but are spelt differently and have different meanings, for example to, two and too. Homonyms are identical words that have different meanings. Examples are: we paid little interest to the interest rates; minute particles of grit had caused the minute hand to slow; the wind-up lantern had been blown over by the wind.

hyphen (-)   This is a punctuation mark that joins two related words or clarifies the meaning. Examples are: a wind-up torch; a ten-year-old child; a light-blue coat; fifty-two pupils; self-addressed envelope.

inverted commas   *See* speech marks.

mnemonic   A rhyme or acronym used to aid memory, for example 'i before e except after c'.

nouns   These are the name of a person, place, or thing. Proper nouns start with a capital letter, for example: Prime Minister, Westminster, Tuesday. Collective nouns, for example team, use a singular verb.

oral test   This is a test of spoken communication skills.

paragraph   This is a chunk of text covering a single topic or theme in one or more sentences.

parentheses (brackets)   A pair of brackets used to insert additional information into a sentence without interrupting its flow.

participles   The present participle is the -ing form (eg working, playing) of the verb and the past participle is the 'ed' form of the word (worked, played). Many past participles have irregular verbs (eg teaching becomes taught, eating becomes eaten, singing becomes sung).

phrase   This is a group of words that form part of a sentence but without the verb necessary to form a complete sentence.

positives   These are adjectives that describe one noun.

possession   *See* apostrophe.

prefixes   These are placed at the front of a root word to give it the opposite meaning. Examples are: un-, dis-, re- and non-, as in unnecessary, displease, rewrite and nonessential.

prepositions   Short words such as in, or, by, at, for, that link a noun (or pronoun) with the rest of the sentence.

pronouns   Words used instead of nouns, for example he, it, you, your.

prose   This is a passage of text.

punctuation   Marks used to break up sentences and clarify meaning.

redundancy   This is the mistake of saying the same thing twice, as in first priority, jointly together, close proximity, SATs tests.

root   *See* sentence stem.

semi-colon (;)   This is punctuation used to mark a pause that is longer than a comma but shorter than a full stop. For example to link two clauses without using a conjunction, as in the following example: She gained a First Class degree; the final essay had been easy.

sentence   Starting with a capital letter and ending with a full stop, they contain a verb and a subject to express a complete thought.

sentence stem   You are given the first part of the sentence and have to choose the best ending from the alternatives given.

speech marks (" ")   Punctuation used to indicate direct speech.

suffixes   These are placed at the end of a root word to change its meaning or tense. Examples are -ed, -en, -ing, -ful, -es, -ous and -ize.

superlatives   These are adjectives that compare three or more nouns, for example the best of the three teams.

synonyms   These are pairs of words that have similar meanings, for example leave and depart, circular and round, disguise and conceal.

syntax   This means the rules of sentence construction.

tautology   The mistake made when an idea is expressed twice in the same sentence. *See* redundancy.

tense   In grammar it refers to verb tenses that describe the past, present and future.

verbs   These are words that describe the action being done.

vowels   The speech sounds a, e, i, o and u.